Improving the Healthcare Dialo

Contents

ABOUT THE AUTHOR

Becoming aware at a time of great hope and great fear formed his outlook, the wonder years, the sixties. Around him there were people with memories of World War II still fresh in their minds but not discussed. Images of emerging movements like the Peace Corps, Civil Rights contrasting with old practices like canned goods in the basement and "duck and cover" at school. There were many dilemmas - War, peace, love... communists, hippies. Boys watching footage of Vietnam in shop classes, being prepared for the tasks they would be drafted to undertake in a few years. The horror in learning of the holocaust, an aunt that was haunted throughout her life of the news of December 7, 1941 or an island hopping Marine hero that once, and only once, brought out his captured Japanese flag – this was the milieu of his time growing up.

Then there were assassinations and a moon landing, the inception of Medicare, scandals, sex and conspiracies along with the characters of the time like The Beatles, Walter Cronkite, John Lennon, the Kennedys, Nixon. Reflecting on events like Kent State, Woodstock, Helter Skelter, Summer of Love and the 27 Club. He was the tail end of the baby boomers.

Hope or fear? The author chooses hope; pursued a dream to be a scientist and to be in service to those in need. "Ask not what your country can do for you…"

After graduating from a public university he worked at Brigham and Women's Hospital in Boston as a Medical Technologist in the blood bank. He went on to be a research assistant and carried this skill to Los Angeles. He attended another public university, received an MBA and set out on a career of healthcare information technology. He worked as an analyst, consultant, project manager, director, executive director and vice president. His career went from mainframes to networks to the electronic medical record. Along the way learning, in addition to technology, the politics and operations of our healthcare delivery system. With 40 years of experience and an engaging personality there is no other better suited to translate the complexities of healthcare for those simply seeking life, liberty and the pursuit of happiness.

FOREWARD

The current discussion on healthcare involves lawmakers holding up in committees, coming up with ideas and voting the party line. These representatives will not have to live by the plan. The only "skin" they have in the game is getting re-elected.

In Congress 35% of the House of Representatives are lawyers, 51% of the Senate are lawyers *(Congressional Research Services)* while 0.36% of the general population are lawyers. *(www.denniswpottslaw.com)* There are 535 elected representatives between the House and Senate. How many understand healthcare? How many understand insurance? How many have listened to what people want?

In the spring of 2017, the House of Representatives passed a bill numbered1628. It was dead on arrival in the Senate but it is interesting to see what the House considers important. For example: Title I Subtitle C - Repeal of the Tanning Tax. Or Title I Section 114(a) Reducing State Medicaid Costs by disenrolling high dollar lottery winners. We actually paid our representatives to come up with the idea. It is a short bill 126 pages. *(www.congress.gov)*

A recent opportunity allowed for time to spend traveling and talking with individuals throughout the country. One person at a time, I present three questions designed to be open-ended:

1. What do you think of healthcare?
2. Do you know the difference between Medicare and Medicaid?
3. Is healthcare a right or a privilege?

Making no mention of political parties, countries nor asking for individual stories... the task is to look for a perception with the intent of finding the lowest common denominator to start a meaningful discussion with the hope of treating this important issue with the respect it deserves. I invite you to consider if the current dialogue represents logical thought. How can this be improved? Perhaps we need better questions.

Assumptions were made that the current and past presidents would be mentioned, and that blue states would be different from red states. These assumptions were incorrect. A commonality brings us back to the Declaration of Independence, a need for Freedom, a strong work ethic and a generosity for those that follow this ethic.

"The fact that disease and injury deprive many Americans of the opportunity to fulfill these rights because they were born in the wrong place, or because their families could not pay the price, denies our belief that men and women are created equal and should have an equal opportunity. Disease and injury can strike any of us - it is a matter of good or bad fortune. Disease and injury can leave any of us broken both physically and financially because we did not get good health care and paid dearly for what we did get." *(US Senator 1972)*

As you read, please take a couple of words of caution. First, it is always easier to make something more complex. The challenge is to do the hard work of making things simple to understand, the lowest common denominator. Second, stay focused, we have many problems. This book will stay focused on healthcare.

CONGRESS

So many people expressed frustration with Congress that some even made me promise to comment on that issue in this book. I found no better words that those listed below.

George Washington's farewell address
Saturday, September 17, 1796

"However [political parties] may now and then answer popular ends, they are likely in the course of time and things, to become potent engines, by which cunning, ambitious, and unprincipled men will be enabled to subvert the power of the people and to usurp for themselves the reins of government, destroying afterwards the very engines which have lifted them to unjust dominion."

Washington is warning the American people against the negative impact that opposing political parties could have on the country and worried those future political squabbles would undermine the concept of popular sovereignty in the United States. Essentially taking power from the people and putting it in the hands of the few.

Without mentioning this quote, the perception is many people feel this is true of our current political state. How can all the republicans agree and all the democrats agree but on different things? A few outliers break party

7

boundaries, very few. Do our representatives have independent thoughts that go beyond party/money lines? Do you feel represented? Perception is reality.

In the spirit of those that forget are condemned to repeat, history that is, let us look at the formation of these parties. The Democrats trace their lineage back to 1792; it is the oldest party in the United States. The Republicans a bit later let us say about middle of the 19th century, definitely by the time Lincoln was president. It is worth noting that a third party, The Progressive Party, had Theodore Roosevelt as President from 1901 to 1909. This explains what got him a place on Mount Rushmore alongside our Founding Fathers and Lincoln.

What each party has stood for has changed over the years. At its most basic and going all the way back to the framing of the Constitution there always seems to be a group of politicians that have favored a strong central or federal government and another group favoring a weaker federal government and more power for the states. In the late 1700's it was easy to tell them apart, there were the Federalists and the Anti-Federalists. Today the Democrats would relate to the Federalists and the Republicans the Anti-Federalists...I guess...

The debate over healthcare to some degree reflects this division with the added elements of a discussion between government control and the free market. The problem is the government is already deep into the healthcare business with about 56% of all funding coming from our taxes via governmental programs. In addition, to make matters even more complicated, that 56% is then split between the States and the Federal government. What have we done?

Regarding "free markets", we exist in an environment that by law restricts competition for our for-profit or commercial insurers. Health insurance is regulated by states and this has meant significant state variation in the rules governing insurance companies and the health plans that they sell. Some states have numerous requirements mandating coverage of certain benefits, while others have taken a hands-off approach to benefit design.

Opposition to the "free market" approach includes the notion that insurance companies would incorporate in a state whose laws were lenient allowing that company to offer lesser benefits and potentially choose the healthiest members. Those for the "free market" suggest allowing national sales of health insurance would increase competition and allow for the development of products more focused on health than sickness, save money and

9

lower premiums. There needs to be a discussion about how to create a "free market" independent of individual state control. Federalist or Anti-Federalist? Does it create confusion for you that the Reds (Republicans) essentially want to override state control of insurance? Does this go against their Anti-Federalist leaning? Blues (Democrats); are you paying attention?

The Affordable Care Act (Obamacare) addressed two major problems that will help create a better environment for the "free market" The Act did this by adopting national standards for health plans. 1. You cannot be denied insurance for pre-existing conditions. 2. Establishing a nationwide minimum set of benefits that need to be provided by every insurance company. These are large strides towards health that are under appreciated. Should Blues and Reds be able to agree on this? At least see it as a starting point for healthy discussion?

 Still outstanding is age discrimination where we are charged higher premiums based on age, if you're between 60 and 65 you're in for a big unpleasant surprise it you don't have employer based insurance.

What is insurance anyway? Let us understand some basic concepts.

Insurance is a way to protect against unexpected events that could result in a personal or corporate financial disaster. It allows an individual, policyholder, to pool resources with others that have a common concern about these unexpected events. The policyholder pays a premium and hopes never to use the benefit. Inevitably, someone in the pool has an event, let us say a house burns down and the insurance company pays $200,000 to rebuild. The policyholder has been paying premiums for 20 years at $2,000 per year, or $40,000 total. That is far less than the cost of the rebuild. If everyone in this pool were to have a house burn down the insurance company would soon be out of business. However, there is only a very small chance that everyone's house will burn down. Mathematicians, known as actuaries, have calculated, based on prior experience how many houses might burn and set a premium based on that calculation.

Let us talk more about these "pools". Known by insurance as "Risk Pools" they are the group of insured people. Generally, the larger the pool the less risk simply due to sheer size but it is also about the make-up of the pool. In our burnt house example if the company only insured houses near areas prone to wildfires the premiums would have to be very expensive, probably unaffordable. The insurance companies want a mix that will limit the risk of everyone's house burning to provide an affordable premium.

The same is true for healthcare. In a perfect world, a health insurance company would want to insure all the young, healthy, and affluent because the old and the poor are going to be the most expensive. The old and the poor tend to use more healthcare resources. A big difference between home fire insurance and health insurance is we are all going to need healthcare at some point; it is just a matter of how much. Is there a moral imperative to insure everyone?

There has always been money involved with getting elected but the intent was, once elected do not make a career out of it. With the honor of election, you serve the people and return to the "farm" after your term of work is completed. Somewhat akin to jury duty.

Now let us turn to a current day icon. In a 2011 interview with CNBC, I invite you to consider; that Warren Buffet modernized the thoughts of President Washington's farewell address. At that time, he referred to it as the "Congressional Reform Act of 2011"

1. No tenure and no pension for congress.

Congress collects a salary while in office and receives no pay when they are out of office.

2. Congress (past, present and future) participates in Social Security.

   a. All funds in the Congressional retirement fund move to the Social Security system immediately.

   b. All future funds flow into the Social Security system and Congress participates with the American people. It may not be used for any other purpose.

3. Congress can purchase their own retirement plan, just as all Americans do.

4. Congress will no longer vote themselves a pay raise. Congressional pay will rise by the lower of CPI or 3%.

5. **Congress loses their current healthcare system and participates in the same healthcare system as the American people.**

6. Congress must equally abide by all laws they impose on the American people.

7. All contracts with the past and present Congress are void effective 1/1/12

   a. Congressional representatives made all these contracts for themselves.

b. Serving in Congress is an honor, not a career. The Founding Fathers envisioned citizen legislators, so ours should serve their term(s) then go home and get back to work.

This is how you fix Congress...

AMMENDING THE CONSTITUTION

The above will require an amendment to the constitution. It is not easy to do, but it can be done in two ways. One is that an amendment is introduced by Congress and is approved by both houses with a 2/3 majority. The other is for the legislatures of 2/3 of the states to call for a constitutional convention. Either way it then must be ratified by 3/4 of the states. The second method has only been used once, in 1787 to produce the current constitution. The President has no say in this process. *(Article V of the US Constitution, from the National Archives)* There have been 27 amendments.

It takes time to go through this process of writing the amendment, getting 2/3 majority votes, and involving 3/4 of the states to get it ratified. The shortest time for an amendment to be ratified was 3 months and 8 days. Put in place on July 1, 1971 it changed the voting age from 21 to 18 years old. *(wikipedia)*. Remembering this as a public outcry from the young, "I'm old enough to fight and die for my country but I can't vote..." This happened fast due to public pressure pointing out it is the right thing to do. It also had no impact on Congress.

There was also some reference to the drinking age, some states reduced it to 18 then changed it back to 21 after the Vietnam War. Apparently, the drinking age is not a constitutional issue; it is left up to the states.

On May 5, 1992 the latest, the 27th amendment was ratified. Submitted on September 25, 1789 it took 202 years 7 months and 10 days for ratification. It had to do with Congressional pay raises. This is the record for the longest time for an amendment to be ratified. *(wikipedia)*

On March 24, 1947 Congress did act on term limits by submitting an amendment to hold the President to 2 terms. It passed on February 27, 1951. *(Wikipedia)* What are the chances Congress will propose an amendment limiting their own terms?

Public pressure...

There, promise held to those generous enough to spend time discussing the issue of healthcare. Hope it did not disappoint. Moving on to the 3 questions...

15

WHAT DO YOU THINK OF HEALTHCARE?

Question 1

Against her mother's instructions Barb borrowed a bathing suit and from her cousin to swim in a public pool. Within two weeks, the Doctor drove her to Boston where she spent 2 months in an iron lung. Her sister, Louise, could not attend school and the house had a red sign in front: CAUTION POLIO! Allowed to return to school after Thanksgiving, Louise caught up with her studies and graduated in 1939. Barb had a relapse in her 60's. She died a week shy of 78. Louise has yet to get polio... *(as told by my 96 year old cousin Louise)*

Although tangential, it is interesting this story came out of our "3 question" conversation. Now more to the point is a summary of question 1...

"We need it. It is important - do not have it you are going to die. People that do not take care of themselves do not deserve anything. People need to be more willing to take a job they consider beneath them."

The above being out of chronology let us start at the beginning of this endeavor. My last two jobs were at

University of California San Francisco Medical Center and Stanford Healthcare. Both had a shorter run than hoped. I questioned myself, my relevance. It is difficult not to, being made redundant twice in as many years.

Most of my career was in healthcare technology but to be successful you need to have a deep understanding of the operations of how healthcare is delivered. It was no longer acceptable for a nurse or a physician to say, "I'm computer illiterate". For a long time, not being able to use a computer was said with a sense of pride. I had to learn how things work to help caregivers adopt digitization.

With my role in healthcare technology no longer center stage in my career I decided to turn my attention to the patients, the community, the funding, and politics. After 40 years there are still large gaps in my knowledge, healthcare in the United States is so complicated. How could a person on the outside of the industry begin to understand it? How can we have so few people in Washington deciding they know it all? Presenting only 2 solutions, a red one and a blue one. Maybe there is a purple one.

I love exploring this country and decided to do some listening in search of how to help with this critical issue. I packed the car in the spring of 2017 and hit the road.

The first challenge was winter storm Ursa. Plans to camp and mountain bike were set aside to deal with snowy roads and cold temperatures.

Words from the road; some thoughts to consider....
Question 1: What do you think of healthcare?

"The latest attempt got lost in the details. Derailed by a lack of understanding and lack of caring. How can you care when it doesn't affect you..." *(random millennial)*

"Scared to use healthcare because of the high cost of co-pays and deductibles" *(dental hygienist)*

"Everyone has to pay before healthcare will work. Your premiums are crazy high between 60 and 65" *(dentist)*

"It would cost me thousands each month if I didn't have insurance" *(young diabetic)*

"Go to prison...get healthcare" *(facebook post)*

Just a note on technology, you know I am going to do it...

Two people are herding a group of cattle on horses and two others on dirt bikes. The horses appear much more efficient in the loose soil with no paths. *(eastgate Lone)*

Temperatures are going to be in the low 20's tonight, opted for a motel.

Next morning...

"Why don't we have free healthcare like Canada and England. We would pay more in taxes but it wouldn't break us." *(motel clerk)*

"Physicians are in it for the money; they take kickbacks from drug companies and do unnecessary procedures" *(motel maid)*

Thomas French appeared at a combination gas station, store, motel and casino that is at least 100 miles from the nearest small town. Fighting the cold and snow he looked weather beaten, all his possessions in a baby jogger. As we started discussing the weather his mission became apparent. He has walked about 22,000 miles in his life, yes walked, and here he was in the middle of nowhere walking to Philadelphia from San Francisco. His goal is to get to 25,000 lifetime miles, the circumference of the earth and this current trip should do it. Look him up, Thomas French, Casper Wyoming, originally from Oakland California. He

19

has also done some canoeing, and helped start a music festival.

His thoughts…

"Obamacare wanted sweeping reforms but didn't get them. Should have held out to get what he wanted"

"Universal healthcare 10 years from now"

"It will be political suicide to eliminate healthcare from 25 to 30 million people that now have it"

"Now isn't perfect but it might get better"

"I'm technically for universal healthcare, we're going to pay a tax, why not pay extra tax, and socialist thinking might not be bad"

"Wyoming doesn't want it"

"Today it's not universal, it's affordable"

Thomas talked about an x-ray he received in Oregon. The physician's advice about the soreness in his ankle; do not walk anymore. Not very helpful when walking is your life.

AM radio is alive and well. Going through Utah heard about a program called MediShare *(www.mychristiancare.org)*

Stated as not insurance but a way for people that agree on a certain lifestyle to share medical expenses. A controversial idea at best, thought it was worth a quick mention, the link is there if you have more interest.

Had to head north to avoid my traveling companion winter storm Ursa. It was closing portions of interstate 70. Plotting a path to stay just behind it and hope for the best. What happened to spring?

Talked to a man with a disabled son, he had a lot to say about healthcare but what I remember most is his story about how his father, a policeman, handled a motorcycle gang that showed up in his rural town making all sorts of a ruckus. Residents complaining, he was outnumbered and no backup for hours his resolution was impressive.

He approached the gang explaining that folks around here had to work, he said let the fire die down, pick it up again in the morning and you will always be welcome here. An expected response occurred until a gang leader appeared and said let us listen to the man. He did not tell us to put the fire out, he did not tell us to move on. Other towns had the same problem with the same gang and they would ask him how he had no problems. The answer: how did you treat them?

"Healthcare sucks. Before Obamacare it was a lot cheaper" *(gary greenough self-employed)*

The next stop was near the last stand for the Ute Indians in Colorado.

"Healthcare is important. We have good local healthcare, just got a new hospital 2 years ago" *(antique shop cashier)*

Steamboat Springs was not the posh ski resort I was expecting. Arriving during "mud season" means you cannot ski and it is too wet to hike or bike. The motel room had fluorescent overhead lights, interesting industrial touch.

"Healthcare is needed" *(bartender)*

"Now we can capitalize on healthcare. If we make it a law we can't" *(millennial)*

The responses to Question 1 were usually clear requiring very little interpretation. I was not there to challenge people, just listen. Even when I knew what they said was technically wrong I just recorded the thought. The goal is more to find perceptions than realities, for a person's perception is their reality. If we want to change an individual's perceptions we must approach that carefully, nobody likes to be told they are wrong.

The above response: "Now we can capitalize on healthcare. If we make it a law we cannot broke that mold and got me to think and wander down different paths. Instead of clarification, I decided to see where my thoughts would go.

One example of healthcare capitalization is the advertising industry. People are making good money by advertising the benefits of a product or service. This is not about public service ads. We are talking about ads that say buy my stuff and my services, it is better than the other guy's.

Sponsored by Kantar Media Ad Age Datacenter published (October 2016) an article titled "Healthcare Marketing". *(you have enough info to find a copy, interesting read, nice picture of Jennifer Aniston)*

"Buoyed by spending on new prescription drugs and by increased competition among hospitals and other big providers, the healthcare industry in one of the 10 biggest categories of U.S. ad spending – and in the past few years, one of the fastest-growing categories.

An "exclusive" analysis by Kantar Media shows the total U.S. advertising spend for the healthcare industry increased 11.3% in 2015 to $9.7 billion."

The article goes on to say...

"The bulk-86.2% - of healthcare ad spending comes from 2 categories: pharmaceutical companies, which represent nearly two thirds of total spending, and hospitals, healthcare systems and clinics."

Competition is an expensive luxury in healthcare, not a penny of that goes to making people better, and it goes beyond advertising.

The San Francisco Bay Area has Stanford Healthcare, University of California San Francisco, Kaiser, John Muir Health System, Washington Hospital, Tenet, all competing for the same population. In business, you call it a "zero sum game". All having beds and clinics to fill, all with different administrators, all with different information technology departments, all with different marketing departments... In a "zero sum game" you are not looking to meet a growing demand. Instead, you take patients away from one hospital to fill your beds and by doing this you hurt your competition because they cannot fill their beds.

As a kid, never saw an ad for the local hospital or the polio vaccine. Compared to the $3 trillion annual spend on healthcare advertising is a drop in the bucket. This does get me to wander down another path. What if there is already enough money in healthcare and we are not spending it wisely? More on that later. In the meantime, if there is enough money in the system, please do not focus on just one part. There will be plenty of blame to go around to pharma, insurance companies, providers, consumers and of course the government.

It seems that mountain passes are optional for snowplows. It can go from relatively clear to your car floating on large sheets of ice and snow just by going around a bend. Oh Ursa, I grow tired of your company.

Weary from the snow and with an appointment on the East Coast, my mission was to make tracks. Ego almost got the better of me as I decided to outrun Ursa, get ahead and flip her off in the mirror. Fortunately, my remote navigator that helped plan stops and work around the storm talked me out of it. I will be forever thankful to her because the next morning, not a mile down the road I encountered a menagerie of spun out trucks and cars littering the side of the highway. It was now May and that was the last day of snow but the cold would linger.

Resuming Question 1 on a cold rainy day in a public house on Cape Cod seemed a bit hypocritical given what we know about the impact of alcohol on health. At the same time, it all felt historical as you can find many references to the pub being the "Crucible of the American Revolution".

Bruce, a retired self-admitted conservative had this to say…

"Canadian system seems to work – best system I've heard of. You have to wait 6 months for an MRI but you get your medicine for free."

MRI (Magnetic Resonance Imaging) is a test that reveals details about the inner workings of the body that a traditional X-ray cannot. They are very expensive to install, maintain and use. You will find Canada's MRI shortage in the literature, maybe they have too few. If Canada has too few maybe we have too many. I worked at a small Children's Hospital in the San Francisco Bay Area that had 2. I don't know how many are in the Area in total. If you are not using them, you are losing money. I bet a Canadian Doctor could jump the line for a life-threatening situation.

Bringing up Canada is a slippery slope for a healthcare writer. We have compared our system to other countries. By many measures, including life expectancy and costs, we are not doing a good job; at least we are not the best. Talking about these statistics does not seem to move the agenda forward, so I am not going to talk much about other countries. Regarding Canada, I do not know enough about their system to be for or against it and I will venture a guess most you reading do not know either.

I can quote stats on the number of MRI's around the world from our Center for Disease Control (CDC) in Atlanta Georgia. Bottom-line, I do not know what the right number is; I do not think the CDC does either. How about: what can we afford? Look if you want, there is a lot of credible information on the web and most people can tell the difference between credible and bull.

I invite you to consider our healthcare spending is focused on sickness, not health. A healthy population does not need a lot of MRI's.

Should an analysis of other countries be input into how we are going to approach healthcare? Should we attempt to learn from others? At present, we only have two choices blue or red and both are a mess. May I suggest again, purple? What are the pros and the cons? Isn't this how analysis is done?

About this time, Mrs. Black from the Committee on the Budget reported the bill House of Representatives (H.R) 1628. Although everyone knew it was dead on arrival it does give insight as to how our Congress works. Check out Title I subtitle C – repeal of the tanning tax and Title I section 114 (a) – reducing Medicaid costs by stopping high dollar lottery winners from receiving benefits. Easy to find (https://www.congress.gov/bill/115th-congress/house-bill/1628) and an easy read. It is worth a chuckle. If it were submitted as a high school project, I would give it an F and ask about drug abuse. The Senate could not improve it and has seemed to give up even trying.

"Both sides have to lose to get anything done" *(unknown source)*

Back to Question 1...

"Healthcare sucks. I pay $400 per month for individual Blue Cross Blue Shield and I still get billed as if I didn't have any insurance." *(natty)*

"Twisted an ankle, physician said I needed an MRI but I don't have enough money" *(natty)*

"Doctor said he would write a note to take time off from work while I recover. The problem is I don't have a corporate or state job... if I don't work I don't get paid" *(natty)*

"People without money that don't work get free treatment" *(natty)*

"Most important issue of our day" *(don p)*

"We spend all this money and still don't have the quality of service" *(don p)*

Meeting Don added the personal economic dimension. To sustain this project requires money and that is where he wants to help. The first order is to complete this book then figure something out.

"You put away for retirement but it will really go for healthcare" *(maryland)*

"Healthcare is in flux, it has to be stable for the economy to grow" *(pennsylvania)*

In West Virginia Question 1 generated a discussion about how Verizon is trying to get a retired worker on Social Security disability so Verizon does not have to pay for her health insurance. Finding this unbelievable further questions revealed they Verizon has even offered to provide her with lawyers. *(k&k)*

West Virginia was one of the most enjoyable stops of the trip. Staying at a hotel used primarily by oil and infrastructure workers provided a sense of community I did not expect. A common shift was to work 21 days on then drive home to another part of the state for 4 days off. An industrious couple provided a mobile cheese steak and pizza trailer to offer variety in food choices. The hotel also provided dinner 3 nights a week, a less attractive but still good option.

Many choose to hang out outside even with an impending thunderstorm. The conversations were easy and it felt like an old time general store where the locals would meet and catch-up on current events. I tried the 3 Questions a couple of times but most of these workers were tired and wanted to rest before another 10-hour shift.

"How are we going to afford all this?" *(kevin)*

Then there is the unexpected response. What do you think of healthcare/

"Educational" *(forgotten)*

Took me off guard, one of the few times I asked for elaboration….

"You get out of it what you put into it" *(forgotten)*

Like the previous answer regarding capitalizing on healthcare it was time to let the mind wander. Perhaps this is about personal accountability. Being a participant in the healthcare system is not a passive activity, we must participate in our own health. If you research how to be healthier and how to respond to any unfortunate sickness: Will you get more out of healthcare?

More thoughts from the road…

"It's out of control. Insurance companies created a monster by paying what was asked" *(herbert)*

"I'm a diabetic, type 2, there is a cure but it's not being released because there is too much money involved in the treatment." *(herbert)*

"How many tests do they have to run?" *(herbert)*

The last response brought back memories of a recent New Year's when I probably had the flu. Being out of town, I went to the local urgent care clinic believing I needed antibiotics. Not being a big fan of overusing antibiotics, this was a big step, but the illness had been going on for at least a month. The physician listened to my lungs, all good, probably the flu and nothing more. Then he recommended a battery of tests and an X-ray. When I asked the purpose, he responded, just to make sure. This seemed excessive and I refused. He offered a flu test. If it was $20 I probably would have done it just out of curiosity but he said it was probably over $100 and would not change anything. Educational – it should not be the more money I put into it the more useless information I get out of it. Are we doing too much?

"Healthcare is a scam. A relative isn't 65 and she has a $6,000 deductible" (lineman)

"How can insurance companies survive when I can sign up get a hip replacement then drop the insurance after my recovery. They (insurance companies) only get a few months premium for a very expensive operation" *(insurance salesperson needing a hip replacement)*

"Can't afford to be without it, costs me $1,800 per month" *(castle)*

"Cheaper today, it all depends" *(drawbridge)*

"Hate it right now, doesn't really help, very expensive" *(kingstable)*

"If you're on state assistance you get everything paid for... if you're a senior you don't get everything paid for" *(kingstable)*

"Obama didn't do enough to help people that needed the help" *(kingstable)*

"With Trump, I don't know what's going on" *(kingstable)*

"Get people that have welfare and four kids jobs" *(kingstable)*

"You want to get more money, have another kid" *(kingstable)*

"People need to work for healthcare. Will someone take better care of a car that is given or one that is earned" *(specialops)*

"What if we went to a 2/3 majority vote in Congress" *(specialops)*

"They are career politicians" *(specialops)*

"Coverage for pre-existing conditions is good" *(specialops)*

"We look to the government to take care of us. Historically this has created a cycle of freedom to bondage and back" *(specialops)*

"It's messed up, I like my doctor because he looks at it from a natural perspective" *(malta)*

A shop owner in South Dakota talked about the Enchanted Highway. A 32-mile stretch in southwestern North Dakota that includes 7 completed (2 in progress) scrap metal sculptures. Making it a collection of world's largest scrap metal sculptures. Gary Greff is the artistic genius and is found most days at the Enchanted Hotel located on the southern end of the highway. Gary's inspiration is fueled by the desire to bring life back to the town where he grew up. The hotel is in the old school and the sculptures are impressive in their beauty and size. *(please do not associate any comments with the artist this was a non-working stop)*

During this trip, I did not use a GPS and only occasionally Google Maps. Instead, a good old paper map and directions from locals helped me on the way. Technology will find you the quickest way between 2 points, not the most interesting.

From here it was onto the Hi-Line of Montana. I learned the term Hi-Line on this trip. The reference goes back to the Great Northern Railway. It is a related to highway 2 that runs 30 to 50 miles south of the Canadian border. A very common reference for this area and you will see it in a business name, for example: Hi-Line Gas.

Thoughts from the Hi-Line…

"I'm fine with national healthcare" *(fredsue)*

"On the ride through Canada I saw some poor kids but they had healthcare" *(fredsue)*

"Canada has reasonable rates, good healthcare" *(fredsue)*

"Why not take a look" *(fredsue)*

"Obamacare was created by people that didn't know anything about healthcare" *(fredsue)*

"Dumbass politicians spend time on stupid things" *(fredsue)*

"Now high rates, $1,200 per month, with high deductibles" *(fredsue)*

Others soon joined Fred, Sue and I as the conversation in front of the store continued. A delicate conversation began regarding "how equal are we?" I cannot sing, others can. Looking at it based on skills, inherited, or learned, we are not equal but we should not be condemned for our unique talents and everyone should have equal access to healthcare.

There is a perception in the country that the percent of people that do not want to work is increasing. Lot of Canadian AM radio on the Hi-Line. Rush Limbaugh is very hard on the millennials, describing them as basement dwellers living off their parents.

Using Rush Limbaugh in reference to Canadian radio is unfair. There is a diversity of programming I found refreshing. There was talk of Native American issues, the pipeline, farm products, events and news. Recently a

35

Canadian sharpshooter in Afghanistan neutralized a target from 3 kilometers, a record for Canada. There was national pride and a discussion about the unfortunate circumstances that require such actions.

Back to the road…

"If it's national and we all have the same we haven't created an incentive to work" *(fredsue)*

"Growing my business is tough, if I go above 50 employees the expenses aren't worth it, my company is stunted" *(fredsue)*

"Easiest way to get a good program is to have the politicians use the same plan, Social Security too" *(fredsue)*

A brief moment to discuss Social Security; the following came out of context to the discussion but I believe it is important. *(fredsue)*

"We keep talking about when Social Security is going to run out of money even though we pay into it. When is Welfare going to run out of money? *(fredsue)*

"How can we make plans when this expensive component of our lives is an unknown" *(fredsue)*

As I prepare to wrap up this section on question 1 you will notice, outside of a Dentist, the questions were purposely posed to individuals that do not work in healthcare. The responses recorded are raw, no explanations simply wanted to put down the words as close to what was said as possible. Just trying to define a perception.

With that said, there are two more interviews where we break from this mold. The first is feedback from a Physician. In addition to practicing medicine he has spent time administering payments to doctors and hospitals. The second is from a medical biller who deals every day with trying to get bills paid for doctors, hospitals and patients.

Now the work of simplification gets difficult because of the need to introduce the healthcare reality of "Cost Shifting". Fair warning what you read may sound insane, because it is. You may not believe it but it is all too true. Sad is the fact that when it comes to how we pay for our healthcare, it is the tip of insanity, but if you can understand the tip, at least you will know there is an iceberg.

It is doubtful that many members of our Congress understand "Cost Shifting"; it would be fantastic to hear them explain how we solve it. If you believe it, you will agree it does need solving.

To start let us break healthcare reimbursement into 3 categories. 1. The government uses our taxes to pay bills through two programs, Medicare and Medicaid (more on this in the next chapter). 2. Commercial insurance companies like Aetna, Cigna, United, etc. also pay healthcare bills. 3. The patient pays directly. Known as co-pays and deductibles, and the occasional very rich person that does not have to worry about money.

Somebody that has a deeper knowledge of insurance can confuse the above by talking about different programs and plans, do not listen it all rolls up to one of these 3 categories. Fight complexity and embrace simplicity.

What the government pays is low when compared to commercial insurance companies. If a hospital or provider were to rely solely on the government, they would go out of business...out of business. This is where the Commercial insurance companies come in. To make ends meet hospitals and providers overcharge Commercial insurance to make up for the losses caused by low government reimbursement. In other words, they shift the cost.

How could this be? Are Commercial insurance companies that stupid? This is done with everyone's knowledge except the patient's and probably Congress. Think about it, in addition to our taxes paying for government healthcare those of us paying commercial premiums also subsidized government healthcare. There is nothing hidden. Commercial Insurance puts up with it because they could select the healthiest individuals. Prior to Obamacare, they did not cover pre-existing conditions; all their members in the prime of their life and most would probably not need expensive treatment. By the time their members reached an age where using healthcare is more likely those members will be shifted over to the government's Medicare. Commercial was willing to pay because they did not want to touch the poor or the elderly.

Income and age have impacts on health. The government covers the poor and the old while Commercial insurers avoid this risk by agreeing to pay higher rates for covering a more favorable population. "Cost Shifting" (www.healthaffairs.org).

You will find debate regarding if cost shifting really exists. (kaiser family foundation) Going back to our discussion on insurance and risk pools it is clear that cost shifting is an important thread holding our fragmented reimbursement together.

The poor, the old and the commercial. If we believe the poor is the Medicaid population and the old is the Medicare population, well both pools are far more likely to use healthcare than those that have jobs and are relatively healthy, this is the Commercial pool. What essentially our government has done over the years is used "adverse selection" to create a pool of people that are very expensive to insure. On top of that, the commercial insures did not have to insure anyone that was already sick. Why would any for-profit rock this boat?

The Affordable Care Act (Obamacare) messed that all up by making it a law that pre-exiting conditions must be covered. Moreover, to add insult to injury the law also had a minimum list of benefits. Commercial insurance is responding with higher premiums and thousands of dollars in deductibles that each patient must cover. The issue of cost must be fixed.

Regarding cost, let us look at the 20 million people that now have an insurance policy. Part of the Obamacare minimum benefits say an insurance company must provide preventative care to stop small problems from becoming bigger and more expensive problems. Prior to setting this minimum benefit people would go without care until the situation became so bad they had to go to a local emergency room. The emergency room is a very expensive way to receive care that should have been done in a Doctor's office. Imagine the cost savings if we can prevent a certain amount of people from having to go to the emergency room.

"Healthcare is a mess because funding is totally chaotic" *(physician)*

"Instead of one source, there are multiple sources all doing their best to cost shift to someone else." *(physician)*

"The plan being considered by Congress is to defund Medicaid to decrease the cost to government but care will still be provided, just more inefficiently, at higher cost, borne primarily by hospital emergency departments who in turn will over charge insured patients to cover the loss. Insurance companies will raise rates so that insurance becomes less affordable so more people are uninsured, again increasing costs to hospitals and the whole cycle goes around again." *(physician)*

"Commercial plans are big money makers for a select few executives" *(medical biller)*

The average compensation for CEO's in the top 20 Commercial health insurance companies in 2015 was $20.5 million. (www.beckershospitalreview.com)

"Commercial reimbursement rules are changed frequently and seemingly are purposely made to be complicated to

the average person, often delaying or denying payment"
(medical biller)

"Even the customer service reps for Commercial insurance, who are primarily outsourced to another country, have trouble understanding the rules. *(medical biller)*

"The rules for government reimbursement are far more consistent and understandable, rules are widely communicated and customer service reps are based in the US and know how to help their members." *(medical biller)*

"Now we can capitalize on healthcare. If we make it a law we can't" *(millennial)*

Above is a repeat of a comment made in Steamboat Springs. Talking about commercial insurance triggered a thought that helped make sense of this comment. In addition to understanding the difference between commercial and government reimbursement, let us talk about the difference between public companies (for profit) and not for profit companies.

Let us keep it simple, a public company is traded on a stock exchange such as the New York Stock Exchange (NYSE) or NASDAQ. Feel free to look up the translation of the latter acronym but in today's society I find it is sometimes better just to accept it as a word.

When a company goes "public" it agrees to sell shares of the company on one of these markets, let us say the NYSE. Then people (investors) agree to buy these shares, if they find the price acceptable. These investors essentially own a piece of the company. Some investors only own a few shares others can own large percentages of the company.

The reason this matters in healthcare is that the shareholders bind public/for profit companies to maximize shareholder value. Shareholder value means a monetary return on their investment, simply put ... make more money. Suppose this for profit company is considering closing a hospital that is losing money. The closing will harm the worker's and the local community but it will benefit the shareholders. The shareholders will win this battle. *(S. Bainbridge April 2015 New York Times)*

Humana and Tenet run hospitals, are for profit and you can buy their stock from the NYSE. Most hospitals are run as not for profit, the technical description of a not-for-profit is a 501(c)(3) corporation. That description if provided for interest, you do not need to understand it for this discussion.

In the spirit of simple, there are two things you need to know about non-profits. The first is a common misconception that non-profits cannot make money. They must generate a modest profit to afford buying new medical equipment, building new buildings and new programs that benefit the community. The second is by law they are required to report on how they benefit the community they serve.

Where for-profits serve the shareholders, non-profits serve the community.

"Woe is me that should even whisper the notion of socialized medicine. All credibility and fortune shall be lost."

Before I redact the above words that "shall not be spoken" let us point out that non-profit corporations, of all kinds, are as much a part of our national fabric as for-profits.

A 2009 article published by Forbes "Capitalist Case for Nonprofit Health Insurance" is worth a look.

"If you want to know what went wrong with our healthcare system and the best way to fix it, all you have to do is look back a few decades to a time when health care was a community concern, considered as essential as any public utility. It should be again, not just because it makes sense but also because it's the most profitable way to go."

"...when Wall Street (NYSE) discovered there was money to be made turning nonprofit health insurers, hospitals and nursing homes into investor-owned companies. What we got was a massive conflict-of-interest profit vs. public good that has culminated in a dysfunctional health delivery system that has undermined our economy, reduced our national wealth and torn our social fabric."

Last I checked Forbes is more conservative than liberal. Perhaps John E. Girouard went rogue with this article and has since been censured.

A reminder, I am not looking to present the solution because I do not know it. The intent is to present questions that can be used to construct a useful dialogue. Questions that should be at least considered, before Congress constructs a plan in a vacuum of both input and knowledge.

United Health Group, Anthem and Humana are examples of for-profit healthcare. Kaiser, Harvard Pilgrim and Tufts are examples of non-profit healthcare organizations.

Now to question 2...

DO YOU KNOW THE DIFFERENCE BETWEEN MEDICARE AND MEDICAID? Question 2

We do not give the Millennials enough credit. Debates over climate change, uncertainty over healthcare, cost of education, sending jobs overseas, cost of housing and then there are the politicians. Are there any leaders left in the world? People providing guidance and hope, saying it will be ok and we believe them. We leave the millennials as perhaps no generation has been left... go figure it out yourself and good luck; we have our own problems.

I once said that I would rather have my kids play a violent video game than watch a political advertisement. Why you ask... because it can be explained that the video game is fantasy where the political ad is reality.

Back to the task at hand. Do you know the difference between Medicare and Medicaid? It can be argued this question may not be as unbiased as intended. We talked about the government reimbursement being fed through one of these two programs. Given that a large part of healthcare expenses are paid for through the government perhaps, we should understand the basics.

All numbers below are from the Centers for Medicare & Medicaid Services (CMS) website unless otherwise noted.

If you go to www.cms.gov you will find CMS described as "a federal agency within the United States Department of Health and Human Services(HHS) that administers the Medicare program and works in partnership with state governments to administer Medicaid. "

The above description is valid but one could argue that CMS is so much more. It is really not; this is what the agency is supposed to do. If it is doing "more" then why is it doing that? Where to it stray from its mission? I hope the simplify theme is starting to come through. It can be made very complicated but let's continue the search for the lowest common denominator and we'll start with how much did the US spend on healthcare in 2015 (latest figures available)

In 2015 the US spent $3.2 Trillion in one year on healthcare.

I just realized my calculator could not handle trillions.

www.census.gov reports the US population at 323 Million

That is $9,920 per person per year.

Of course all the numbers above are rising.

Now let us break this down into the two categories I have described commercial insurance (referred to as private health insurance in CMS spreadsheets) and government, or better stated taxpayer dollars.

In 2015 we spent $1 Trillion on Private (Commercial) health insurance.

In 2015 tax dollars supported $ $1.8 Trillion in government reimbursement.

If you check this out on cms.gov, you will see how it is more complex by the addition of more categories, read the footnotes the above number is what our tax dollars fund as government healthcare reimbursement. If you add the above 2 numbers you will find we are missing about $400 billion that needs to be accounted for to make it to $3.2 Trillion. You will find that in a category "Out-of-Pocket Payments". This means that in addition to what the government spends, in addition to what commercial insurance spends, we, as individuals still have to kick in another $400 Billion. (www.cms.gov table 3)

Our tax dollars already fund 56% of all healthcare

Numbers like this are all over the place and usually just generate useless noise. I wonder how many in Congress can quote these numbers without asking a staffer. Maybe they are too busy to remember all the details but the feedback from the country is this is a critical issue, if not the most critical issue, facing our time. One way or another we need to get this resolved and move on.

I will return to the topic of costs but let us get back to the trip and find out what people know about Medicare and Medicaid. You will be saved from more laments regarding winter storm Ursa. Well maybe just one more: it put up a good fight but in the end, I prevailed.

Question 2 – Do you know the difference between Medicare and Medicaid?

"I don't know the difference" *(lawyer)*

"One is for healthcare the other is for retirement" *(random millennial)*

"I don't know the difference" *(young diabetic)*

"Medicare is for the elderly and doesn't cover everything. Medicaid if for people on welfare and it covers everything, including dental." *(motel clerk)*

"I don't know the difference" *(thomas french)*

"Social Security we pay through our payroll taxes, Medicare we pay through our payroll taxes, but don't really know the difference." *(gary greenough self-employed)*

"Medicare is for the elderly and Medicaid is for the young, special needs and disabled" *(antique shop cashier)*

"I don't know the difference" *(millennial)*

"Medicare is what I paid for. Medicaid is what I'm paying for" *(bruce – self admitted conservative)*

"I don't really know" *(natty)*

"Medicare is what I get. Medicaid is if you do not have any money. If you own a home put it is your kids name or the government will take it" *(cousin louise)*

"Medicaid is like welfare, when you don't have anything. Medicare is what you pay for all your life." *(don p)*

"I have to sign up for Medicare when I turn 65 even though I have retirement healthcare paid by my employer. Why do I need it? Guess it's for a catastrophe" *(k&k)*

"It's income base. Medicaid is for when you have nothing and it pays for everything. Medicare is when you get old and it limits what you pay" *(forgotten)*

"Not really" *(Herbert)*

"Medicaid is for the indigent, Medicare is an entitlement because we paid for it" *(lineman)*

"If you can't afford healthcare you get Medicaid. Medicare is for when you get older" *(insurance salesperson needing a hip replacement)*

"Medicaid is for any age" *(castle)*

"Medicaid is state assistance and you get everything paid for. Medicare is for seniors and you don't get everything paid for" *(gift store)*

As with Question 1 I am not going to record all the answers. Patterns develop and the above is probably enough to establish a pattern on Question 2.

Overall, I talked with about 300 people over 6 months. Yes this is anecdotal, as intended. Generally, I like interacting with people and am always learning to be a better listener. Not all the conversations were about healthcare. Many were front porch, general store kind of discussions about the weather, kids, sports, news etc. At one time, it was called "chewing the fat" and was done face to face not face to phone.

I enjoy learning the origins of phrases such as "chew the fat", and they can be difficult to trace. This one may have come from sailors chewing on salt hardened fat while resting and conversing. *(wikipedia)*

Out of 323 million people, this is most certainly not going to pass a statistics test. It was never intended to. It is meant to form a perception based on interactions with people and applied against 40 years of healthcare business experience.

Redundancy is a great teacher and memory aide. With that spirit: finding the lowest common denominator around which we can have a meaningful and productive discussion about healthcare is the goal. How can Congress breakdown this massively complex problem so we the people can understand how the decisions are being made and the impact of those decisions on our lives.

To get to a decision you need a plan. Plans can be used to communicate. If you agree with the plan it can provide comfort, if you do not it can create anxiety. Even if you do not agree with the plan, at least you know it, can comment on it, and try to change to plan or adapt to the circumstances.

Uncertainty in our lives is always there, who knows what tomorrow holds but where we can throw an anchor let us do it. Healthcare does not have to be one of the uncertainties. I invite you to consider, it should be an anchor. Whatever the Congress decides there will be one less unknown, one less variable that we need to wonder about. We still may worry but at least we can develop our personal plans.

In addition, it will not just reduce a variable in our lives, think businesses, our jobs, how we put food on the table and a roof over our heads. Currently businesses do not know what to expect. All they know is there a huge expense that affects planning and the health and happiness of their employees and Congress cannot even make it predictable.

Each Congressperson gets $174,000 a year plus benefits plus a pension while the average household salary is stated to be about $51,000 per year. Even with this seemingly generous Congressional pay package, you will find at least one recently retired (2014) representative, Jim Moran complaining it is not enough. _(www.npr.org)_ To be fair, it is doubtful many of our elected representatives are this tone deaf but this seems to be better than a living wage for a job that should be an honor.

Message to Congress – get your act together and start doing your job.

Message to Citizens – get your act together and start sending emails, or something.

"In a democracy the people get the government they deserve" (Alexis de Tocqueville)

Back to Question 2…

For the people that did have a notion about the programs the following two quotes seem to capture at least the perception if not the reality of the differences between Medicare and Medicaid.

"Medicare is for the elderly and doesn't cover everything. Medicaid if for people on welfare and it covers everything, including dental." *(motel clerk)*

"Medicare is what I paid for. Medicaid is what I'm paying for" *(bruce – self admitted conservative)*

If you accept that 56% of healthcare comes from the government and most of that through Medicare and

Medicaid perhaps we should better understand these programs. I will keep it to just the important points and at a high level. It is easy to complicate this matter and politicians love to complicate, it keeps them from having to answer the questions.

If you have sat through a lengthy Power Point presentation you can probably relate to the sleep inducing, crowded with word slides that go on at nauseam, often leaving the audience tired, confused and with little time to ask questions.

KISS is an acronym for "Keep it simple, stupid" as a design principle noted by the U.S. Navy in 1960. The KISS principle states that most systems work best if they are kept simple rather than made complicated; therefore, simplicity should be a key goal in design and unnecessary complexity should be avoided. *(wikipedia)*

For the purposes of this discussion, I invite you to accept the below definitions...

Medicare

Medicare is an insurance program. Medical bills are paid from trust funds. These trust funds are collected with each paycheck and put into a trust (an account) with the federal government. We pay for Medicare every day we work. It serves people who are over 65 whatever their income, and serves younger disabled people and dialysis patients. People on Medicare pay part of costs through deductibles for hospital and other costs, like drugs. Small monthly premiums are required for non-hospital coverage. It is basically the same everywhere in the United States and is run by the Centers for Medicare & Medicaid Services, an agency of the federal government.

For more information regarding Medicare and its components, please go to http://www.medicare.gov.

Medicaid

Medicaid is an assistance program. It serves low-income people of every age. Patients usually pay no part of costs for covered medical expenses. A small co-payment is sometimes required. Medicaid is a combination federal-state program. Benefits vary from state to state. State and local governments within federal guidelines run it. To learn more about Medicaid and to see if you qualify for your state's Medicaid (or Children's Health Insurance) program, see: https://www.healthcare.gov/medicaid-chip/eligibility/

In summary Medicare is a federal program, Medicaid is a state program run within federal guidelines. The Affordable Care Act (Obamacare) expanded Medicaid the American Healthcare Act (Trumpcare) seeks deep cuts in Medicaid.

When healthcare cuts are on the table, you will notice Medicare left out of the discussion. Two reasons: One, we pay for it with our payroll taxes and two, people over 65 are a powerful political lobby.

If you can accept Medicaid is the battleground then let us explore that and potential discussions around improvements. "Follow the Money" is a catchphrase from the 1976 docudrama: "All the President's Men". It implies that if you follow the money you will find corruption. I am not suggesting corruption, some always exists and it should be looked at but it should not be the focal point of discussion. Instead, let us "Follow the Money" and look for inefficiencies.

Medicaid is a combination of Federal money and State money. In actuality, it's all our money paid through taxes.

Next, let us look at FMAP (Federal Medical Assistance Percentage). This is the money the Federal Government (Feds) sends to the States to help pay for Medicaid. At its simplest, the Feds will match a dollar for every dollar the state spends on Medicaid. Of course, it is more complicated than a 1 for 1 match but let us not go there today. Therefore, if the goal is to lower Medicaid costs let us follow the money from the taxpayers pocket to the Federal Government back to the States.

It costs money to put money in motion. First, the money must get to the Feds via payroll tax. Somebody has to account for this money then somebody at the State has to fill out some kind of form to get the money back. Having personally filled out these types of forms it represents a lot of work, a lot of time and time is money.

Question for Congress:

"If Medicaid money is going to go back to the States anyway, why send it to the Feds first?"

As the money travels, each agency/department that touches it will reduce the total dollar amount by paying salaries and benefits, rent on the office space, computers, software etc. Ultimately leaving less for actual healthcare. It is like trying to carry water in a sieve.

There are at least two agencies in Washington that touch a lot of healthcare tax dollars. One is the Department of Health and Human Services (www.hhs.gov) with a 2018 proposed budget of $1.1 Trillion with 80,000 employees.

The other is the Center for Medicare & Medicaid Services (www.cms.gov) with a 2018 proposed budget of $738 Billion with 4,100 employees. Total of $1.8 Trillion and 84,100 employees and this is just at the Federal level. Do not try to tie these dollars back to our overall national healthcare expenditure of $3.2 Trillion. I have tried and that would require another book and a completely different approach to research. Instead, let us put our representatives to work and ask them some questions.

Questions for Congress:

"Why do we have HHS and CMS?"

"What does each agency do?"

"Do these 84,100 employees provide direct care?"

"If they are not providing direct care what do these employees do?"

"What other departments receive healthcare tax dollars that are not included in the above?"

If you are so inclined to ask these questions do not take a complicated answer. Make Congress work for it. This is an important issue and they should be able to provide answers that can be understood by people that do not work in healthcare or politics.

Ok, this $1.8 Trillion rolls around in Washington and there needs to be rules in place so that some of the money makes it back to each of the 50 state's Medicaid program. Unfortunately, if you dive into the details the rules are not consistent, not as easy as a one for one match. Developing and following these rules is expensive and of course, they are constantly changing.

Within each of the 50 States Health Departments need to be there to request, accept and disburse the money. These 50 departments called overhead or administrative expense, not a penny of this overhead goes to pay providers (physicians and hospitals) that actually deliver care. Each State develops, follows and maintains its own rules. Eventually some of the money goes to pay providers.

Customization vs Standardization. We have 50 customized Medicaid assistance programs.

Questions for Congress:

"Why does each state have a different Medicaid program (customization)?"

"Would any money be saved by having each State follow the same rules (standardization)?"

Now, finally the money is getting to the providers. This means a bill for care is submitted and that bill has to be paid. That means we have 50 different billing offices following 50 different sets of rules. By definition, we have redundant processes. Maybe this is a potential area for cost savings.

Hospitals across the country are combining into larger Health Systems so they can leverage size into cost savings. When University of California San Francisco took over Children's Hospital Oakland among the first events was a consolidation of billing offices.

Question for Congress:

"Do you think there is a potential to save money if we consolidate Medicaid billing offices?"

Congress is not without the ability to make suggestions. I refer back to the bill currently being bantered about in the Senate - H.R. 1628. Remember I described the plan to reduce Medicaid by eliminating high dollar lottery winners. You really should look at it, it is a hoot.

By the way, even if the President signs this Bill, or some other like it, it is doubtful the debate will be over. It will just be kicked down the road for the next election. It will only end when representatives stop voting the party line sit down and do the hard work of figuring this out.

Shifting back to Medicare for a minute... The perception in this country is Medicare is an efficient and valuable program. Let us assume that to be the reality.

Question for Congress:

"Given the government already spends $1.8 Trillion on healthcare how much more would it cost to cover everyone through Medicare?"

Knowing that we spent about $10,000 per person on healthcare in 2015 and still did not insure everyone let us multiply that $10,000 times the entire population of 323 million. Surprise we get $3.2 Trillion and everyone is insured. The winners will be the American people the losers are the Commercial, for profit insurance companies. How much are we wasting on the convoluted reimbursement mechanisms that benefit only a few?

Questions for Congress:

"Do you receive donations from for profit health insurance companies?"

"Do you receive donations from drug companies?"

"We are already into healthcare for $3.2 Trillion per year. I invite you to consider Medicare as an option, and if you do not want to consider it, why not?"

Our National Parks are a symbol for everything that is right about this country and our government. Until recently, I did not even know there was a Theodore Roosevelt National Park. Covered in grassland and badlands, it is stunning.

One morning I drove a scenic loop that included prairie dog towns. Prairie dogs are squirrel like creatures that live in a community of holes in the ground. When you walk through a town most scatter into their holes but a few remain above ground to chirp warnings. These guards stay near their hole and will run down them if you get too close.

Before getting out of the car for a hike, some were scampering on the road with one lying still. Fearing it had been hit, but upon closer inspection, it jumped up and ran away. Looks like it was sleeping on the road to capture the leftover warmth of the payment on a chilly morning.

Sleeping on the road, putting your life in the hands of others, trusting they will not run over you. That is a lot of trust I do not have. We cannot be caught sleeping in the road.

To end this section let us talk a little more about the dollars. You have been presented with high numbers provided by CMS but there is plenty of detail with enough inconsistencies to question if we really know how much we are spending on anything. Maybe it is an impossible task. Should we try to establish some baseline dollars that everyone, red and blue, can agree on?

IS HEALTHCARE A RIGHT OR A PRIVELEGE?
Question 3

Not being the first to pose the question, I do not remember hearing any real discussion about this, let alone an answer.

"We are the wealthiest nation on earth and the only advanced nation without some form of nationalized health care. There is no excuse for this." *(physician)*

When asking Question 1 everyone had something to say and responded as if they had been thinking about this and were waiting for someone to ask. Question 2 generated a bit more puzzled looks. Eventually I prefaced it with "I'm not trying to put you on the spot…it's a difficult question most people can't answer". Question 3 tended to generate the most thought. As if the mention of rights and privileges, although being recognized as very important, have not really been given any deep thought, but all agreed it certainly deserved some thought.

"By 1787, the union between the states was unraveling. To save the young nation, delegates from 12 states met in Philadelphia and, with George Washington presiding,

created a new form of government."
(http://www.mountvernon.org)

No, you did not catch a typo. In 1787 only 12 of the 13 states sent representatives. Being so distrustful of the potential for a powerful federal government, Rhode Island refused to participate.

Intending to replace the Articles of Confederation (our nation's first constitution) 55 state delegates met in Philadelphia in 1787. This Constitutional Convention created the 7 articles of our current constitution and the often-quoted 52-word preamble that is below.

"We the people of the United Sates, in order to form a more perfect union, establish justice, insure domestic tranquility, provide for the common defence (defense), **promote the general welfare,** and secure the blessings of liberty to ourselves and our posterity, do ordain and establish this Constitution for the United States of America." *(www.constitutioncenter.org)*

This was written towards the end of the convention. The first 15 words most of us recognize the first 3 are ingrained in just about everyone. Such a simple introduction to such a powerful document that changed, and continues to change, the world. How many of you have read the Constitution? Dare say, I have only just recently read it even though we have all been presented with many opportunities to do so. It is not long. Maybe we should put aside Facebook, Twitter and LinkedIn, just for a moment…

You will notice "promote the general welfare" is highlighted. Can you guess why? We have many people studying the document and we call them constitutional scholars and lawyers. This is the beauty and the curse of simplification, the exact intent is not always apparent but it provides an excellent framework for discussion. We have been discussing the Constitution for over 200 years. May these discussions continue for at least another 200. Below is a table of contents for the Constitution.

- Preamble
- Article 1 – The Legislative Branch
- Article 2 – The Executive Branch
- Article 3 – The Judicial Branch
- Article 4 – The States
- Article 5 – Amendment
- Article 6 – Debts, Supremacy, Oaths
- Article 7 – Ratification

Logic would dictate that to accomplish such a historic feat it must have taken a long time. The constitutional congress of the time proposed the convention in February of 1787, on May 25, 1787, it convened in Philadelphia and on

September 17, 1787, the new constitution was sent to the States for ratification. It became law on June 21, 1788 when New Hampshire became the 9th of the 13 states to ratify. *(www.constitutioncenter.org)*

Just over a year, very quick. If we to attempt this today you could argue that back then there were only 55 delegates from 12 states. In those days, the speediest forms of transportation were the horse and the sail. Each draft had to be hand written, copies were hand written, and the document itself was handwritten. Today we have the world of private jets, cell phones, email, the Internet and photocopiers.

Somehow, I made it through 18 years of school without actually reading the Bill of Rights. The first 10 amendments of the Constitution came about because of a disagreement between the Federalists and the Anti-Federalists. Federalists being for a strong Federal government the Anti-Federalists taking the other side. Today we would probably have the Federalists for Medicare and the Anti-Federalists for Medicaid. The Anti-Federalists sentiment on the constitution is reflected in the statement below.

"Many of the rights and liberties Americans cherish—such as speech, religion, and the right to fair trial—were not enumerated in the original Constitution drafted in

Philadelphia Convention in 1787, but were included in the first 10 amendments, known as the Bill of Rights"
(www.constitutioncenter.org)

Ratification, nor implementation was a sure thing. Those annoying Anti-Federalists needed something to go along and that something is now known as the Bill of Rights. Introduced on September 25, 1789 they were ratified on December 15, 1791.

Below they are listed with actual wording and presented here as an aid to help us determine if there is a place for healthcare in the Constitution. Remembering in the preamble: "promote the general welfare"

THE BILL OF RIGHTS

1 of 10: Congress shall make no law respecting an establishment of religion, or prohibiting the free exercise thereof; or abridging the freedom of speech, or of the press; or the right of the people peaceably to assemble, and to petition the Government for a redress of grievances.

2 of 10: A well regulated Militia, being necessary to the security of a Free State, the right of the people to keep and bear Arms, shall not be Infringed.

3 of 10: No Soldier shall, in time of peace be quartered in any house, without the consent of the Owner, nor in time of war, but in a manner to be prescribed

4 of 10: The right of the people to be secure in their persons, houses, papers, and effects, against unreasonable searches and seizures, shall not be violated, and no Warrants shall issue, but upon probable cause, supported by Oath or affirmation, and particularly describing the place to be searched, and the persons or things to be seized.

5 of 10: No person shall be held to answer for a capital, or otherwise infamous crime, unless on a presentment or indictment of a Grand Jury, except in cases arising in the land or naval forces, or in the Militia, when in actual service in time of War or public danger; nor shall any person be subject for the same offense to be twice put in jeopardy of life or limb; nor shall be compelled in any criminal case to be a witness against himself, nor be deprived of life, liberty, or property, without due process of law; nor shall private property be taken for public use, without just compensation.

6 of 10: In all criminal prosecutions, the accused shall enjoy the right to a speedy and public trial, by an impartial jury of the State and district wherein the crime shall have

been committed, which district shall have been previously ascertained by law, and to be informed of the nature and cause of the accusation; to be confronted with the witnesses against him; to have compulsory process for obtaining witnesses in his favor, and to have the Assistance of Counsel for his defence (defense).

7 of 10: In Suits at common law, where the value in controversy shall exceed twenty dollars, the right of trial by jury shall be preserved, and no fact tried by a jury, shall be otherwise re-examined in any Court of the United States, than according to the rules of the common law.

8 of 10: Excessive bail shall not be required, nor excessive fines imposed, nor cruel and unusual punishments inflicted.

9 of 10: The enumeration in the Constitution, of certain rights, shall not be construed to deny or disparage others retained by the people.

10 of 10: The powers not delegated to the United States by the Constitution, nor prohibited by it to the States, are reserved to the States respectively, or to the people.

Written over 200 years ago, the language can be a little thick but I am not here to interpret as you can find many credible sources on the web that will happily provide you with their opinion.

The first two are the amendments are most often discussed with the 5th being the third most likely to be quoted as "I plead the 5th".

The 5th reminds me of a high school party that I had the ill fortune to chaperone. For some reason, still unclear, a couple of parents decided to rent a local hall and have a "fundraiser". All invitees were below drinking age but guess what ... alcohol made its presence known. When the police were called, they handled the situation with a great deal of tact. The offer to the troublemakers was simple: we will call your parents and they can come pick you up here or do not call your parents, we will arrest you and your parents can pick you up at the police station in the morning. Seemed very fair, but one lad seemed to lack the ability to get in touch with his parents. Demonstrating patience, the officers tried multiple numbers with no avail. The teen then "pled the 5th" and refused to say anything else about his parent's whereabouts. This got him handcuffed and a ride in a police car. Lesson learned: make sure you understand your rights.

Anyway, back to topic. I would not mention it with the question but sometimes during a conversation, I would mention amendment 6 and refer to the right to counsel, a lawyer, public defender. In addition, if I really wanted to lead the conversation I would mention that if we commit a crime we have the right to a free lawyer, what happens when we get sick? Ok, I have preached an attempt at impartiality, just an attempt. Please accept the intent is to have a better discussion about healthcare. I am ready to accept what 2/3 of the people can agree on.

It may be useful to understand what medicine was like during the early years of our country. For this let us refer to the 1982 book written by Paul Starr and titled "The Social Transformation of American Medicine". Below is a paragraph from Chapter 1 – Medicine in a Democratic Culture, 1760-1850.

"The family, as the center of social and economic life in early American society, was the natural locus of most care of the sick. Women were expected to deal with illness in the home and to keep a stock of remedies on hand; in the fall, they put away medicinal herbs as they stored preserves. Care of the sick was part of the domestic economy for which the wife assumed responsibility. She would call on networks of kin and community for advice and assistance when illness struck, in worrisome cases perhaps bringing in an older woman who had a reputation for skill with the sick."

73

It is doubtful the Constitutional Convention gave much thought to healthcare as a right; it was being taken care of.

Starting in 1846 with the first use of ether for a surgical procedure a great disruptive change occurred. With pain free surgical interventions healthcare expanded, made more discoveries, more expansion and has taken over a large percentage of our economy. To participate, to receive care, is it a right or a privilege. Let us see what people think...

"Maybe it shouldn't be in the Bill of Rights but everyone should have it" *(motel clerk)*

"Healthcare is defined as a privilege, seems like it should be a right" *(thomas french)*

"It's neither, just the right thing to do" *(bruce – self admitted conservative)*

"On your own and good luck, the government views it as a privilege" *(natty)*

"Never thought about it. I think it should be a right. People in prison get too much" *(cousin louise)*

"Should be a right" *(k&k)*

"A right if you have been gainfully employed and financially productive to the United States" *(forgotten)*

"Privilege. If you don't' try to work and be productive why should we give you healthcare" *(Herbert)*

"Privilege. It's my job to take care of myself" *(insurance salesperson needing a hip replacement)*

"Privilege. You have to earn it" *(castle)*

"A right" *(gift store)*

"It's a privilege, like buying a house, be careful of the rights, they can be taken away, laws can change" *(specialops)*

"I pay my premium, should be a privilege but everyone should be able to get it" *(farmers)*

"Urgent healthcare, yes but you should take care of yourself and be preventative" *(repairman)*

The Bill or Rights was put in to protect from an aggressive federal government exerting too much control over an individual. In the spirit of welfare, as referenced in the constitution, let us propose amendments 28 and 29.

28. Any health insurer must provide services regardless of a person's current or pre-existing condition.

29. Any health insurer must provide a minimum list of benefits. This list will be from time to time revised under the supervision of the Secretary of Health and Human Services.

Health insurer is defined as a state or commercial carrier.

All right, we provide the above guarantees and have increased competition from insurance companies by allowing sale of policies across all states. Going back to our insurance salesperson looking for a hip replacement… What is going to stop him from changing insurance company's right after he gets that expensive surgery? Nothing is, the same way he can change insurance companies after totaling a car or having a house burnt down.

THE LOWEST COMMON DENOMINATOR
PART ONE

So what does this all mean? Reflecting on recent activities there may not be one common denominator, but perhaps it is time to define this term further. Let us talk about common denominators. There are two ways to look at this the first is from a mathematical point of view.

When two or more fractions have the same denominator (the number on the bottom) they have a Common Denominator. We can add and subtract fractions only when they have a common denominator. For example, we cannot add 1/3 and1/2 but we can represent these fractions as 2/6 and 3/6. The fractions maintain their original meaning but we now can that 1/3 +1/2 is 5/6. Through simplification, it became possible to answer a question that at first appeared difficult. (www.mathsisfun.com)

The second way to look at it is as a trait, characteristic, belief, or idea that is or common to or shared by all members of a group. For example, Dedication to the cause of freedom was a common denominator of the American revolutionaries. (www.dictionary.com)

77

I will now attempt to paraphrase, without prejudice, what people said, with the intent of presenting to those in power what it important about healthcare. This is a tall order given I have already admitted to being human.

1. Everyone should have access to healthcare.
2. It needs to be affordable for all citizens.
3. Everyone should contribute as a productive member of society to the best of their abilities.
4. Those that make the rules need to live by the same rules.
5. No one person or organization should profit excessively by exploiting the sickness of others.
6. Learning from others is a strength not a weakness. This applies to both other countries as well as blue learning from red and vice versa.

A favorite professor in business school would present each new concept with the phrase: "I invite you to consider..." Such a gentle way to ask people to open their minds.

Incorporating all the information provided by the road, my own research and opinions were driven in certain directions. It is time to apply 40 years of experience and express some common denominators for you to consider

1. To Congress: very few people will believe you have done a good job if you do not live by your own laws. One way to end this debate is have Congress participate in the same healthcare program you develop. The consequence of not doing this will be a continual cycle of uncertainty that will stagnate progress for persons and organizations.

2. The complex systems of paying for healthcare need to be streamlined through standardization. Standardization is a common practice for elimination of costs. "You can have any color you want, as long as it's black". *(Henry Ford)* This statement may get the hackles up on many people. I am not talking about healthcare treatment I am talking about standard payment mechanism and standard benefits.

3. People need to take more responsibility for their own healthcare. The best medical advice I ever received came from my mother "listen to your body". Important note; she never made it past the 8th grade, she had to go to work to support the family. While modern medicine performs daily miracles, we all should take part in these miracles and face the realization that sometimes the

miracles do not occur. With active understanding of ourselves and learning how to use the healthcare systems we have in place, I am convinced we can afford healthcare by using the money that already exists in the system better. I am not saying everyone will do this but for those of us that can this is what our country needs us to do. We cannot become the "prairie dog sleeping in the road". This becomes very important if you accept the country being split as to whether this is a right or a privilege.

4. You may have heard "Tort Reform" mentioned in reference to healthcare. This is the concept that a victim's damages are limited when there is a bad outcome in the treatment process. While incompetence cannot be tolerated and needs to be punished, we also need to understand the human body is very complex and that with the best efforts things can go wrong.

5. We must finally decide if healthcare is state or federal. For mostly political reasons Medicare will not be touched but the real reason to leave it alone is it is one of the few governmental programs that works. Medicaid is convoluted mess of federal and

state dollars with at least 25% of those dollars going to administrators that simply move the money around, create complicated rules and support duplicate billing and payment processes. If we are going to allow for-profit commercial payers to exist, they must be free of state restrictions and not allowed to insure only the healthy.

6. People get the government they deserve. We must get more active. Voting is not enough. Do you know who your state and federal representative are? *(www.house.gov)* If you do, when's the last time you sent them an e-mail or a letter, given them a call or even stopped by their local office? It does not take much time and if you get together with some of your like-minded friends at the local public house who knows what can happen. I hear too often that it can be politically incorrect to discuss politics. In certain situations, this might be true. It's all about how you approach it, think of the police officer and the motorcycle gang. With the right to free speech, we also have the obligation to use it in a respectful manner, listening and learning, expanding our horizons to use the power of many to develop better questions and even better solutions.

7. Our local member of congress, Mark DeSaulnier, has two district offices that are open from 8 to 5 in addition to an office in Washington. One is just a few minutes from the house. You can also find local offices for your state senators and state representatives. Now if you do go, do not expect to meet your representative without an appointment. Whom you will meet are known as "staffers". These are typically bright energetic kids trying to get ahead and most of them will succeed because they are not afraid of hard work. Do not discount the power of these "kids" they have access to the representative and are often counted on to help understand the issues important to us, the constituents. Treat them, as you would want to be treated.

Another story from the road to illustrate the power of personal appearance...

Traveling close to Canada in a very rural area, about 12 miles up from a planned stop was a border crossing station that defines the term "middle of nowhere". Not interested in crossing the border but very interested in just visiting and seeing what the station looked like and meeting the workers.

There we no lines for people making the crossing, if fact there was no one there at all except border employees. I parked the car on the American side and walked into the Canadian office. Stating my name and that my intent was not to cross but just to say hi and see what a remote crossing looked like.

There were two agents and they looked at me as if I just crawled out of a Martian spacecraft. One agent realizing I probably meant no harm slowly warmed up and smiled. The other sat there transfixed, wondering if he was going to get a chance to use all that terrorist gear. I asked permission to take pictures. I could do that, just not photograph any people. A reasonable request, took some pictures and went on my way to the American side.

On the American side, there was a similar reaction but a quicker warm up because one of the agents knew the people I was visiting down the street. A second agent stayed mostly out of sight and had that same transfixed stare the Canadian agent had.

Understanding their caution and the unusual visit to a very remote area, I was sure to represent myself in a friendly manner. If we do not act like dogmatic fanatics and use kindness, respect and empathy, we can make a huge impact by avoiding technology and making a personal appearance. Yes, it takes time but if it is important to you, the time will be found.

Although not as convenient, we can reach out to all members of congress, regardless of state of residence. Even though they do not directly represent your district, they do represent all Americans.

THE ETHICAL COST OF HEALTHCARE

If you want to move from audience to participant in the healthcare discussion, you have more than enough information to ask good questions of those deciding our fate. You can also use this book to guide your research to further understanding. It is a matter of time and desire. We all have many things to do; putting a shelter over our head and food on the table is the foundation of our survival and can take up a lot of time.

You may be familiar with Maslow's Hierarchy of Needs. In its simplest form, it describes a structure for human success where one "need" must be fulfilled before you move on to the next. In our context, we can look at the first "need" to discuss how healthcare affects our daily lives. The "First Need" is labeled as Physiological.

Physiological needs are the physical requirements for human survival. If these requirements are not met, the human body cannot function properly and will ultimately fail. Physiological needs are thought to be the most important; they should be met first. Air, water, and food are metabolic requirements for survival in all animals, including humans. Clothing and shelter provide necessary protection from the elements. *(wikipedia)*

A bit of a tangent, you will notice Wikipedia has been referenced more than once. Jimmy Wales, the founder states this as the goal: "Imagine a world in which every single person on the planet is given free access to the sum of all human knowledge. That's what we're doing."

I have found this source to be very helpful in my research. It is non-profit and sustained through individual donations. If you look at the bottom of any article in Wikipedia, you will notice the information contained within these articles is well referenced. It is easy, fun to use and gaining credibility. I caution everyone that any source of information is subject to errors, personal opinions, or information provided solely to market something. Wikipedia can make a good starting point and the references can provide other avenues for research. Use common sense and look at everything, including this book with a critical eye.

Back to Maslow's first need of Physiological, or requirements for human survival. Is healthcare a requirement for human survival? Is it needed before we can become contributing members of society? If we do not get sick, we do not need it, but that is unlikely.

With that in mind, let us consider Gross Domestic Product (GDP). This is a common economic term and chances are you have heard this in relation to healthcare. Why is this important?

Think of it as how much the country made in a given year, in dollar terms. It is our national income, or salary, how much money we have to spend without going in debt. To bring it home, you cannot spend more than you make without using credit cards.

Putting aside the credit cards let us say your household lives by the rule we can only spend what we make. Your expenditures breakdown into categories to include housing, food, clothing, fuel and healthcare. Next year healthcare costs are expected to rise by 5.6% (*www.cms.gov*) Good news is you will be getting a raise next year of 3%, maybe. The bad news is all costs are going to increase and we hope it is no more than 3%. If healthcare costs keep growing at 5.6%, a pace that exceeds your raise eventually you will have a tough time putting food on the table.

To the millennials; we need you to speak up for this is another "time-bomb" you will have to deal with if it is not solved now.

Applying the household example to our nation's income or GDP... "Every dollar spent on health care is a dollar that cannot be spent on something else. No set of expenditures can rise faster than the gross national product (GDP) forever." *(lester c. thurow 1985 harper's magazine)* Tough to argue with, that logic and as you can see by the 1985 reference this is not a new problem. Our decision has been to kick the can down the road, maybe the next generation can figure it out... "Let Obamacare fail; it will be a lot easier" *(donald trump as reported by usatoday july 18, 2017)*

And here lies the crossroad between ethics and the economy. Going back to insurance, with home, auto and life insurance there is a defined benefit; the cost of a home, a car, the value of a policy when someone dies. This provides at least one known that makes the cost of premiums easier to calculate. With health insurance, it is quite different. Human nature is difficult to predict, sickness even more so. Sickness can take many forms, new diseases, new cures, genetics and lifestyle.

To mitigate this unknown some health insurance companies put a cap on the total lifetime benefits you may receive. An insurance company may impose a total lifetime dollar limit on benefits (like a $1 million lifetime cap) or limits on specific benefits (like a $200,000 lifetime cap on organ transplants or one gastric bypass per lifetime) or a combination of the two. After a lifetime limit is reached, the insurance plan will no longer pay for covered services. *(www.healthcare.gov)* Is this ethical? Is it necessary?

"Death panel" is a political term that originated during the 2009 debate about federal health care legislation to cover the uninsured in the United States. *(los angeles times august 14, 2009)* Sarah Palin, former Republican Governor of Alaska, coined the term when she charged that proposed legislation would create a "death panel" of bureaucrats who would decide whether Americans—such as her elderly parents or children with Down syndrome—were "worthy of medical care" Palin's claim has been referred to as the "death panel myth", *(berkeley electronic press 2010)* as nothing in any proposed legislation (Obamacare) would have led to individuals being judged to see if they were worthy of health care. *(politifact august 10, 2009)*

A very dangerous term used to inflame the population by putting fear, uncertainty and doubt in everyone's mind. We need to demand more from the people engaged in the dialogue and be diligent in insuring the above does not become anywhere near reality.

A real-life example unfolding today is the newly found cure for Hepatitis C. Our celebration of this success is tempered by the unpleasant cost associated with it.

On October 10, 2014, our government's Food and Drug Administration (FDA) approved the drug Harvoni for use as a cure for Hepatitis C. Until that time, Hep C could be treated but not cured. Treatments usually go on a lifetime but once you are cured, you do not have the disease anymore. No need for continued treatments.

Success is rated as 96% or higher. A company called Gilead makes it and they estimate a cost to cure of $94,500. *(www.webmd.com)* Government dollars and commercial insurers are expected to cover the costs and ethically they probably should. For an insurance company this is like finding out the house you covered that was supposed to cost $200,000 to replace really costs $294,500 and you have to pay it. Nothing you can do about it this year but you bet premiums are going to rise next year and so the cost of healthcare continues going up.

In a recent Wall Street Journal article, *(jan 4, 2017)* a federal judge ordered Pennsylvania's corrections department to provide these costly new antiviral drugs to an inmate infected with hepatitis C, and rebuked the state for restricting inmates' access to the drugs.

Hepatitis C is an epidemic in prisons, but state corrections departments have treated relatively few prisoners because the drugs are expensive, costing about $54,000 to $94,500 per patient.

The new antivirals, sold by Gilead Sciences Inc., AbbVie Inc. and Merck & Co., began hitting the market in 2013 and have higher cure rates and less severe side effects than older treatments. Hepatitis C is transmitted via infected blood, mostly through needle sharing. Chronic infection can cause serious liver damage if left untreated.

The following is an uncredited comment I found referring to the Pennsylvania lawsuit. "Depriving prisoners of treatment is considered cruel and unusual punishment, a violation of the Eighth Amendment to the Constitution, which is why inmates are the only people in the country with a constitutional right to health care." This is obviously meant to inflame and I do not know if it was used in court but it does represent a perception that exists in our country.

Right here is a real life current example of ethical issues that will need to be addressed. It should not stop health care advances but we must deal with it, not just once but every time an expensive advance is made. In this case there is a positive aspect, the cost of the cure, Harvoni, should be more than offset by the reduction in cost for treating the symptoms over an infected person's lifetime. Eventually it will save money at least that is the theory.

The major problem here is that in the Pennsylvania case, a judge made this ruling and it appears to be heading in the direction of all people with Hepatitis C, at least those in prison, should get the drug. Literature shows that it is not appropriate for all cases. You can go to the manufacture's own website (www.harvoni.com) to learn more about the specifics of treatment. Should clinicians at least have some input into the decision? The drug company thinks so. If you have Hepatitis C, or know someone that does, you should go to a Gastroenterologist, not a judge.

Questions for Congress:

"Who profits from expensive medical advances?"

"Who benefits from expensive medical advances?"

This is not a one-time answer unless you are describing a process because advances will continue.

A good example of a thought through guideline for treatment has been produced and made public by a very successful non profit health care company, Kaiser.

https://healthy.kaiserpermanente.org/static/health/en-us/pdfs/nw/nw_Harvoni_Guidelines.pdf

Sorry for those reading off traditional paper and cannot access the link. You can break the search down to avoid typing the whole thing.

CANADA

It was on a camping trip to the Lost Coast of California that I decided to include a chapter on Canada's healthcare system. So many people spontaneously mentioned it that it reminded me of a quote I have seen a few times on Facebook: "Maybe the answer isn't at the beach... but shouldn't we at least look..."

The Lost Coast is an area of California south of Eureka that has remained mostly untouched, almost pristine. Within the last two years a healthy population of Elephant Seals have returned where none have been before, at least in recorded history.

This background provided a chance encounter with a family traveling from Canada that happened upon this unique environment from advice given in a coffee shop; similar to the discovery of the Enchanted Highway. You might find the most amazing things by taking the time to talk, ask questions and have an openness to learn.

In a political context, it would be easy to dismiss me by saying this whole book is about trying to get Canada's health system into the US. When in reality what I am saying is let us learn from others. We can learn from many sources, other countries included, pick a source, it is very time consuming and expensive when you start from nothing. We may not find any help but our representatives "should at least look".

As we were enjoying a campfire and watching the fog roll in I decided to use a sample size of one and ask the Canadian couple the three questions.

Question 1: What do you think of healthcare? Expecting an outpouring of thought that was provided by 100% of the previous people questioned the surprise was the blank looks on their faces. Apparently, healthcare was not a top of mind issue. Imagine not worrying about your healthcare. Free to grow companies; take risks without worrying how to pay for your next doctor's visit. They had this and truth be told I am envious.

To be worry free, like approaching infinity, is not possible but thinking about the Dentist's words from earlier: "once you turn 60 healthcare premiums go through the roof". Between 60 and 65, you are in a healthcare limbo, likely to need it but cannot afford it. To bring this to a personal level I am currently 58 and self-employed. What should I do? Figure out how little money to make so I am available for subsidies, assuming they still exist? Use savings to pay for very high "out of pocket" *(deductible and copays)* costs? Alternatively, possibly figure out how to become disabled

95

so I can take advantage of Medicare? The best answer is to make as much money as possible so I can afford whatever comes my way. Being self-employed is a risk, what if this book does not work out? Should I abandoned it in search of a good benefit-paying job? What if the book does work out and I employee others and make a difference for everyone? Healthcare is my biggest worry. Imagine spending 40 years in the auto industry and not being able to afford a car? That is what I am facing with healthcare. An unknown that stagnates the risk-taking culture of our country.

None of the options reduces worry, a worry we have inflicted on ourselves by not being an active part of the discussion. I am not ready to let 535 elected officials decide my fate. To be a Socratic gadfly is an honorable endeavor *(wikipedia social gadfly)* to breakdown the previous arcane reference, I plan to be a pain in the backside with the spirit of making progress to help solve the problem of healthcare in America.

If Canada may have something to offer, like the beach... We should be willing to "at least look."

Let us start by looking at www.canadian-healthcare.org. At first glance, it is not the panacea that some people suggest. In many ways, it is similar to our system but the perception within Canada is much different.

"Canada's health care system is a group of socialized health insurance plans that provides coverage to all Canadian citizens. It is publicly funded and administered on a provincial or territorial basis, within guidelines set by the federal government.

Under the health care system, individual citizens receive preventative care and medical treatments from primary care physicians as well as access to hospitals, dental surgery and additional medical services. With a few exceptions, all citizens qualify for health coverage regardless of medical history, personal income, or standard of living.

Canada's health care system is the subject of much political controversy and debate in the country. Some question the efficiencies of the current system to deliver treatments in a timely fashion, and advocate adopting a private system similar to the United States. Conversely, there are worries that privatization would lead to inequalities in the health system with only the wealthy being able to afford certain treatments.

Regardless of the political debate, Canada does boast one of the highest life expectancies and lowest infant mortality rates of industrialized countries, which many attribute to Canada's health care system."

Let us refresh the concept that perception is reality, even if that perception is technically wrong. If you have had to deal with customers in your career, you know how a customer perceives your service or product is a reality that translates into success or failure. You can do everything "by the book" but if the customer does not feel good, they will not use your service or buy your product.

"Put into an international perspective, however, Canada's system looks to be relatively well liked. A 2011 Gallup Poll found that 57 percent of Canadians felt "satisfied" or "very satisfied" with their access to health care services (in the United States, that number stood at just 25 percent)."
(washington post july 1, 2012)

I have noticed that news outlets can confuse things worse than politicians can. But of course, news today is 24 hours a day as opposed to a half hour nightly show and a daily newspaper. That is a lot of time to fill to keep the advertising money coming. "America needs you Walter Cronkite".

As far as I can tell, Canada's system is as complicated as ours it is just more predictable and people feel better about it.

Please forgive that transgression and I hope you are still reading. My personal belief is that America can do a lot better than any nation on earth with any issue we put our mind to. It is our individual responsibility to help continue this country's greatness, not just sit back and watch others do it to us.

"We must have universal health care. Just imagine the improved quality of life for our society as a whole," he wrote, adding: "The Canadian-style, single-payer system in which all payments for medical care are made to a single agency (as opposed to the large number of HMOs and insurance companies with their diverse rules, claim forms and deductibles) ... helps Canadians live longer and healthier than Americans." *(donald trump – the america we deserve 2000)*

Everyone is entitled to change his or her mind and we should be generous when someone, for a good reason, changes his or hers. However, as recently as this year our President complimented Australia's Prime Minister on their healthcare system. A single payer system...

LET'S START RUNNING HEALTHCARE LIKE A BUSINESS

Let us get back to capitalism and get some old-fashioned business sense into this healthcare mess and a common place to start is with a vision and mission statement. Most companies have both. While not a guarantee for success it certainly helps people understand why you are in business and what it is you expect to accomplish. I propose we do the same for healthcare by getting Congress to present a Vision and a Mission that everyone, red and blue, can agree on. This would mean we know what the target is. We may all have different ways to get there but at least we would have a target.

The target would represent the lowest common denominator. It would reflect our principals as a people, a country. It would tell the world what we are about, what made us great and continues to make us great. A message to our citizens that we care about "life, liberty and the pursuit of happiness..." this is a great vision statement, by the way... "We the people in order to form a more perfect union..." a great mission statement.... by the way....

The aforementioned so simple, so memorable with a few words it describes what we are about and how we intend to get it done.

To do this we must accept that government is going to play a role in healthcare for as far in the future as the eye can see. How it plays that role is what is being debated.

The Declaration of Independence set forth a vision that our country would become independent of foreign rule. We did not need to have the exact plan in place to state the vision; in fact, it is better if you do not. Why is it better? Because without vision you cannot have a plan and a plan must be developed by the many. The more people involved the better that plan will be.

At the point of developing a vision statement, you are describing the future. In a company, you do this to explain to your customers, shareholders, and employees that this is what we are doing. Concise, to the point. It should be something everyone with a stake in the company can understand and get behind. In the case of the United States the vision statement in the Declaration of Independence has stood the test of time, 2026 will mark 250 years.

Let us look at other vision statements that many of us are familiar with…

"I have a dream that my four little children will one day live in a nation where they will not be judged by the color of their skin but by the content of their character." *(martin luther king jr. august 28, 1963 – march on washington)*

The entire speech is about 6 pages long – depending how you print it. Powerful and remembered for a short statement a short vision statement that clearly points to a path.

"First, I believe that this nation should commit itself to achieving the goal, before this decade is out, of landing a man on the moon and returning him safely to the Earth." *(john f kennedy may 15, 1961 – joint session of congress)*

To this day, we still refer to the most difficult problems as a "moonshot". If healthcare is a moonshot it is only because we made it so. Make no mistake going to the moon was about a war, a cold war, and the need to win the "space race". It also provided for a great sense of adventure and brought the country together around a common cause not seen since World War II.

"We choose to go to the moon. We choose to go to the moon in this decade and do the other things, not because they are easy, but because they are hard, because that goal will serve to organize and measure the best of our energies and skills, because that challenge is one that we are willing to accept, one we are unwilling to postpone, and one which we intend to win..." *(john f kennedy September 12, 1962 rice stadium)*

These grand statements altered the course of history and will be remembered long after my generation is gone. I am not proposing we try to mimic grandeur and glory of a King or Kennedy; healthcare can be much simpler than civil rights or a moon shot. We just need to follow these examples and agree on a target so we can take aim at what we are trying to accomplish.

Let us look at the Mayo Clinic's vision statement. "Mayo Clinic will provide an unparalleled experience as the most trusted partner for health care."

How about General Motors, "GM's vision is to be the world leader in transportation products and related services. We will earn our customers' enthusiasm through continuous improvement driven by the integrity, teamwork and innovation of GM people. Becoming the best is an unending journey, a constantly changing destination. But that's where we're determined to drive – one car, one truck, one customer at a time."

Ford… "People working together as a lean, global enterprise to make people's lives better through automotive and mobility leadership."

103

It is interesting that Ford included "mobility" in its vision as it opens up a lot of possibility.

One more... Google... "To organize the world's information and make it universally accessible and useful."

Now let us talk about mission. It can get a little confusing regarding mission vs vision. Do not get caught up in that debate. Let us focus on setting that target. Going back to our founding documents, I describe the Declaration of Independence as the vision and the Constitution as the mission. To put it another way: the constitution describes what things need to get done. It sets a framework for governing and defines basic rights. It avoids many details regarding how exactly things will be done. For example, in Article I section 8 it holds Congress accountable "To establish Post Offices and post roads;" It does not say where they should be, what they should look like or any particulars at all. It simply says that given the importance of communication to our new form of government you, Congress, had better get it done.

It may seem odd that the Post Office is mentioned in the Constitution but not if you think of it as the only way to communicate over long distances. If we started the Constitution today what would be said of the Internet?

Let us end this chapter with a working definition of each to be used in further discussions.

Vision – what is the future state we seek?

Mission – what are the things we need to do to achieve our vision?

Having been through many vision/mission exercises there is one thing in common…it starts at the top. The Chief Executive Officer will bring together key people in the organization to begin the discussion. I would propose this job in government should fall to the President. It is not the President's job to work out the details but it is his/her job to set a direction, a vision of what the future state should be. This should be specific enough to be understood and broad enough so most everyone can agree and engage.

What a vision statement is not: "it's going to be a lot better than Obamacare"

After spending some time looking for a vision statement from either President Obama or President Trump the only common ground is "we got to fix it, it's broken". That is not a vision statement. Then you can find sound bites on tort reform, health savings accounts, choose your own doctor, spending is out of control, cut Medicaid, don't touch

Medicare. Neither red nor blue has done a good job articulating a vision of healthcare.

Can we agree on what is broken? Can we agree on how to fix it?

THE LOWEST COMMON DENOMINATOR

PART TWO

The attempt to pass a healthcare bill in the summer of 2017 has the "red group" struggling to agree with itself. They are searching for the lowest common denominator (www.cnn.com) upon which all the "reds" can agree. Given that is the stated purpose of this book I can certainly get behind what they are trying to do.

The problem is they are searching for that denominator among a small group, and it does not matter if it is the red group or the blue group. Groups that are supposed to reflect the wishes of the entire US population but do not. Going back to how can 50 people all agree on one approach just because they are red or blue.

We need to have a lowest common denominator that reflects the citizens of the US. Our representatives are not holding to their duty or promises.

Let us go back to vision. If we all had a shared vision of what's broken maybe we could start to work on the problem. Currently the best statement of any kind that most people can agree with is the following:

"we got to fix it, it's broken"

In actuality, this is fantastic. Something that more than 50% of all people can agree on. I am not being sarcastic. Something we can agree on is reason to celebrate, head to the public house and hoist a few. Red, blue and all the colors, we have agreed. Parades in the streets a national day of celebration...ok... now I am being sarcastic. Back to reality, for a moment, this can be a brief cease-fire... we do not know exactly what is broken let alone how to fix it. For now, just bask in the moment that we all agree it is broken.

Meetings are a necessary part of any government or business and they can be boring pains in the butt. I quit drinking coffee for a bit, because it was keeping me awake during meetings. The problem is a lack of focus. Everyone wants to solve the problem before it is even defined. "It's broken" ...take a moment and just agree it is broken, do not start talking just to hear yourself. Silence can be powerful; following a process can be productive magic. In short, shut up, listen, pay attention and for Pete's sake find a person that knows how to run a meeting. Perhaps this should be a skill set in Congress. Maybe they can take some training days, go to a kindergarten, and learn how to play nice and share.

This is going to sound, and be, redundant and obnoxious but it is so important to getting the point across and making progress. Know where you are in the process. Right now, we can agree that the state of healthcare is... "we got to fix it, it's broken" This is our lowest common denominator.

In the spirit of redundant obnoxiousness, we have a common platform, let us celebrate. Yes, we have found this denominator but we can stop there. Have to admit, if this is all we can agree on it is very embarrassing. Not something, we want to tell the world, but it is a start.

So what do we do next? How about describe a vision for the future state of healthcare? No more than a few sentences. Remember we are not talking about solving the problem; we are not even talking about defining the missions. I propose something much more optimistic... let us state what we want and through this process define our values, connect with the successes of our past and move forward the great experiment we call democracy.

Our future is not guaranteed, it is something we earn. Look beyond your term, the short stay we all have on this planet and push forward not a problem but a vision of the future. Something that will stand the test of time, as have the Declaration of Independence and the Constitution.

So what can we agree on next? It should be short, and to the point but we must consider it might be longer than 140 characters, therefore, not a Tweet.

Below is an excellent example of what a healthcare vision statement could be.

"The United States of America believes that a civilized and wealthy nation, such as ours, should not make the sick bear the financial burden of health care. Everyone benefits from the security and peace of mind that comes with having pre-paid insurance. The misfortune of illness which at some time touches each one of us is burden enough: the costs of care should be borne by society as a whole. That is why the United States wishes to re-affirm in a new Healthcare Act our commitment to the essential principle of affordable health insurance."

Let us pull this apart, sentence by sentence and see where there could be possible agreement and objection.

"The United States of America believes that a civilized and wealthy nation, such as ours, should not make the sick bear the financial burden of health care."

It should be tough to find an objection to the above. This is why we have an insurance industry.

"Everyone benefits from the security and peace of mind that comes with having pre-paid insurance."

We all share the risk of our house burning down so as not to create a financial disaster for the few that will experience this devastating loss. Knowing that we can provide medical care for our loved ones and ourselves when tragedy strikes can provide a peace of mind that frees us from worry as we go forward to be productive members of society.

What is potentially controversial is the part about "pre-paid insurance". Going back to a statement from the road: "Everyone has to pay before healthcare will work". That is tough to argue, insurance must have a large enough pool of people so that not everyone in that pool will get sick at the same time. We already have pre-paid insurance through work, healthcare exchanges, and Medicare. Medicare is a pre-paid insurance; check your pay stub, it is taken out every pay period. Medicaid is different. Going back to another comment from the road... "Medicare is what I paid for. Medicaid is what I'm paying for". Medicaid is not a pre-paid insurance.

I am breaking my own rule; getting too much into the detail – see how easy it is. Climbing back up to a high level, it is safe to say that everyone has to pay something for healthcare if this is going to work. At this point, we should not talk income and subsidies that is for later. If most agree with this it is time to continue the celebration. On to the next sentence…

"The misfortune of illness which at some time touches each one of us is burden enough: the costs of care should be borne by society as a whole."

The only potential for objection here is the word "society". To some this could sound a little socialistic. In reality, this is a bit redundant to the concept of pre-paid insurance. Take that word out and others will object to what sounds like all private insurance. Might need a little wordsmithing: how about:

"The misfortune of illness which at some time touches each one of us is burden enough: the costs of care should not financially destroy an individual, family or group."

Now we can argue that nobody wants to see someone bankrupt because of excessive healthcare costs. Again, we do not solve it at this step; we are still looking for that lowest common denominator upon which red and blue can agree. Finally the last sentence...

"That is why the United States wishes to re-affirm in a new Healthcare Act our commitment to the essential principle of affordable health insurance."

The only challenge with this comment is the word "affordable" and its connection to Obamacare and the Affordable Care Act (ACA). It is sad that a word can be polarizing. Putting the politics aside, we can all agree it needs to be affordable.

Now let us look at it again in its entirety:

"The United States of America believes that a civilized and wealthy nation, such as ours, should not make the sick bear the financial burden of health care. Everyone benefits from the security and peace of mind that comes with having pre-paid insurance. The misfortune of illness, which at some time touches each one of us, is burden enough: the costs of care should be borne by society as a whole. That is why the United States wishes to re-affirm in a new Healthcare Act our commitment to the essential principle of affordable health insurance."

This proposed vision is used simply as an example of how we could communicate to our citizens, and the world, our values, all in 94 words.   I wish these were my words, but they are not. To provide some mystery I will not reveal who said this until my first talk show interview.

For a moment, imagine we, as a nation, have developed a common vision for healthcare. This would be a great moment in America's history. We need to celebrate but we cannot rest for now it is time to discuss how we achieve this vision.

Introducing the concept of mission, we now must get a little more into the detail and document for all to see, the steps that need to occur. Military analogies are common in business. Using World War II, our vision was to defeat the enemies in Europe and the Pacific. To do this we engaged in many missions. D-day being a very well know mission, the taking of Iwo Jima being another.

What are the missions we need to undertake to finally put healthcare to rest and not have it be a center of attention? Other important issues outside of healthcare also need the attention of the American people. The work becomes more difficult now because we need to start defining problems that stand in the way of our vision. We needed the island of Iwo Jima to establish a base closer to the enemy. D-day was important because we need to get on the European mainland to return freedom and order to Europe.

What are the missions we need to undertake to solve healthcare? From my research, I propose the following.

1. We will insure 100% of the citizens of the United States.

The problem we currently face is that even with current gains we still have 11.3% of the population not covered by health insurance. This is as of the first quarter of 2017 as reported by www.gallup.com. If we use the census count of 323 million Americans that leave 36 million people without insurance, without access to basic healthcare, except through an emergency room. An emergency room is the most expensive way to provide care. There are cost saving potentials.

This is a big problem if we are to hold to our vision statement. Can anyone support that we should have citizens without insurance?

Some good news here is that starting in 2014 we saw a drop in the amount of people uninsured. In 2013 we had 18% or 58 million Americans without insurance. In 2014 the Affordable Care Act (Obamacare) became law of the land. Something in that law made a dramatic change and now the reds want to repeal the whole thing. What? Really? Get rid of the whole thing?

The needle moved in the right direction but still there are problems, we all know that it is not perfect but is there something worth saving, something worth working on?

For once I'd like to hear a red say that blue idea wasn't half bad…we should get together and talk about how to make it better. I would like to hear the same thing from a blue about a red idea. Compromise does not seem to exist across parties and dictatorial rule is the norm within the parties. Looking at it from the outside, I would give both parties a time out until they can share the toys in the sandbox.

Going back to the road: "If you don't have access to healthcare you will die"

Question for Congress:

 "How does your plan insure 100% of Americans are insured?"

Another saying you hear in business that applies to our current state of politics: "Lead, follow or get out of the way"

Any plan that does not insure coverage to 100% of Americans will be a non-starter. In addition, research leads me to the conclusion that Americans are ready pay for this.

You, Congress, figure out a plan; that is what we are paying you for.

If you do not want to insure 100% of Americans then just say so. Come up with a target or criteria that will deem a person worthy of coverage and a percent target of how many should be left without insurance.

2. This insurance will be based on a uniform set of terms and conditions.

Insurance companies already have regulations imposed on them and it is done by the states. This includes health insurance and creates an inequity to the point where one could go "shopping" and move to the state that has the best deal. An extreme statement, perhaps, but if our mission is to cover everyone we should at least consider a federal requirement to meet basic minimum standards? I repeat: "at least consider". What are the pros and cons of having a federal minimum requirement for health insurance? This is a common business practice when making a decision, analyze the pros and cons.

Well the good news is the Affordable Care Act introduces the concept of Minimal Essential Coverage (MEC). To be a "qualified health plan" under the MEC that plan must provide 10 essential benefits. Please Read below...

117

- Outpatient care—the kind you get without being admitted to a hospital
- Trips to the emergency room
- Treatment in the hospital for inpatient care
- Care before and after your baby is born
- Mental health and substance use disorder services: This includes behavioral health treatment, counseling, and psychotherapy
- Your prescription drugs
- Services and devices to help you recover if you are injured, or have a disability or chronic condition. This includes physical and occupational therapy, speech-language pathology, psychiatric rehabilitation, and more.
- Your lab tests
- Preventive services including counseling, screenings, and vaccines to keep you healthy and care for managing a chronic disease.
- Pediatric services: This includes dental care and vision care for kids

This is already law of the land. If you want to get rid of it ok, but will it be replaced by anything or will insurance companies be allowed to define benefits depending on the regulations within each state? Does this seem unfair that everyone must play to this common denominator of minimal essential coverage?

Remember this is only a proposal, something to consider and can easily be replaced by another mission but if we are going to fix healthcare we need missions.

3. It will be portable across all the United States.

State's right vs. the Federal Government, a very long-standing debate. Right now insurance is not portable across states. If you move to another state you are going to have to get new insurance, unless you have Medicare. Definitely if you have Medicaid. Remember that is different in each of the 50 states. It is difficult to reapply and if you have an existing condition requiring treatment a lapse in coverage could be devastating.

Imagine if every state had its own currency and you wanted to visit 5 different states. You would have to convert your current money to 5 different currencies to be able to purchase anything. What if each state was responsible for its own military and in order for the Federal Government to declare war a certain percentage of states would have to agree. How secure would we be? How efficient would that be? Think about 50 Commander in Chiefs.

"We hold these Truths to be self-evident, that all Men are created equal, that they are endowed by their Creator with certain unalienable rights that among these are Life, Liberty, and the Pursuit of Happiness...." *(declaration of independence)*

Where does healthcare fit in? At a state or federal level? If it is not intended to be portable across states then what is our mission?

4. It will provide reasonable access medically necessary services.

I could add to this that access must not be impeded by financial or other barriers. And here lies the rub. It is great to have a grand vision statement and ambitious missions but who is going to pay for this? If we can agree that everyone should pay we that's a start, but how much. Although advances towards the 100% insured rate have been made under the Affordable Care Act we are seeing some flaws. The 11.3% uninsured rate, while lower that the 18% of 2013 this represents an increase in uninsured from the 2016 number 10.9%. One reason could be the amount of co-payments and deductibles each person is responsible for, thousands of dollars a year in some cases. That combined with rising premiums is forcing people out of the market places.

The reds are seeing this, and I hope the blues too. Cutting Medicaid by billions is being proposed. The problem here is that is does not make things more affordable. Throughout my career, I have been in situations where costs must be cut. In the worst situations I have had to deal with what are known as; "across the board cuts", every department has to cut 5%, no real plan from administration just do it. This is a leadership cop-out. Leadership cannot figure it out; they give up and hope for the best. This is what we see the reds doing and the blues are not helping the situation.

Question for Congress:

"Why aren't the blues providing legislation that would improve the Affordable Care Act?"

America spends over $3 trillion on healthcare, approaching $10,000 for every man woman and child in the country. Is this enough? If you believe that healthcare spending exceeding the gross national product is a problem then this simply cannot continue.

Maybe we do need the draconian approach I just castigated. If we cannot come up with a plan then maybe it is time for another Congressional timeout.

In business cost cutting situations, you always start by looking at non-labor costs. Having to lay off people is very difficult and should be recognized as a failure of leadership. Unfortunately, labor is often the biggest cost in any business and has to be considered.

Let us reconsider administrative overhead and breakdown costs into two categories.

1. Direct costs – in healthcare this is defined as the cost of medical supplies, physician time, nursing time, drugs, etc. In short direct costs are associated with care and those costs vary depending on how many patients you see and how sick those patients are. If you have less patients and they are less sick you will spend less money.

2. Overhead or indirect costs – also known as fixed costs. These include non-medical supplies, administrator time, the billing office, information systems, human resource departments, the building itself, etc. These expenses indirectly support patient care but the costs do not vary based on the number of patients seen or how sick they are. They remain mostly fixed, even if the number of patients seen drops dramatically. Because these costs do not directly affect patient care, they are a lot easier to cut than physicians and nurses.

You can lower overhead costs by reducing administrative overhead through consolidation and standardization.

To summarize I humbly present to you a take on the Lowest Common Denominator in the form of a vision and mission statement for healthcare in the United States of America.

"The United States of America believes that a civilized and wealthy nation, such as ours, should not make the sick bear the financial burden of health care. Everyone benefits from the security and peace of mind that comes with having pre-paid insurance. The misfortune of illness, which at some time touches each one of us, is burden enough: the costs of care should be borne by society as a whole. That is why the United States wishes to re-affirm in a new Healthcare Act our commitment to the essential principle of affordable health insurance."

To achieve this vision we will tackle the following missions.

- **We will insure 100% of the citizens of the United States.**
- **This insurance will be based on a uniform set of terms and conditions.**

- **It will be portable across all the United States**
- **It will provide reasonable access medically necessary services.**

Take this for what it's worth and if you care about about the healthcare issue please form your own opinions.

THE ELUSIVE COST OF HEALTHCARE

All the numbers presented can be debated. The primary source is the Center for Medicare and Medicaid Services (CMS), another source is from the proposed 2018 Federal Budget as presented by the US Department of Health and Human Services (HHS), the Congressional budget Office (CBO) and the Joint Committee on Taxation (JCT).

With all humility and 20 years of budgeting experience, I can be considered a healthcare financial analysis expert. Upon arrival at Stanford Health Care, There was a tangled web of no budgets, no way to allocate funds to various projects, no way to project future costs and a very complicated and time-consuming process to get money approved and vendors paid. Upon my departure, this was better under control and at least people started asking good question.

At UCSF, the dollars associated with a merger were without good definitions. I had to ask questions and annoy many people to get to an understanding of what we were planning on spending and what "bucket" that money was coming from and what does that "bucket" mean. For example, there was $125M to spend on information technology projects and a good description of what projects would be done but not a good understanding if all

125

the projects would come out of that $125M. Seemed to depend on whom you asked. There needed to be clarity in order to make progress... a very difficult task.

With that said, let us go back to CMS and HHS and see if we can figure, out how much we spend and what we are spending it on. A good place to start is with Table 3 from CMS; "National Health Expenditures; Aggregate and per Capita Amounts, Percent Distribution and Annual Percent Change by Source of Funds; Calendar Years 2009-2025". Here is the breakdown for 2015, the most recent actuals calculated by CMS.

Category	2015 Actual
Out-of-Pocket Payments	338,100,000,000
Private Health Insurance	1,072,100,000,000
Medicare	646,200,000,000
Medicaid	545,100,000,000
Other Health Insurance Programs	121,100,000,000
Other Third Party Payers	482,900,000,000
TOTAL	$3,205,500,000,000

Now we will move to the proposed 2018 budgets for CMS and HHS and as a way of comparison, we will present the 2018 CMS projections so it is more "apples to apples".

Category	2018 Projected
Out-of-Pocket Payments	382,700,000,000
Private Health Insurance	1,280,400,000,000
Medicare	767,900,000,000
Medicaid	621,800,000,000
Other Health Insurance Programs	146,400,000,000
Other Third Party Payers	546,500,000,000
TOTAL	$3,745,700,000,000

According to this projection, we are now at $3.7 Trillion for National Health Expenditures. Now let us see if we can figure out what each category means.

1. **Out-of-Pocket Payments:** No footnote on table 3 that would explain this. From Medicare.gov, we find the definition: "The Out-of-Pocket Costs (OOPCs) are calculated using the events or incidents of health care usage reported by individual people with Medicare from the Medicare Current Beneficiary Survey". I am confused; is "out-of-pocket payments" just Medicare dollars or all dollars spent independent of insurance? I assume it's all and I also assume it means co-payments and deductibles. Right there are 2 dangerous assumption when it comes to understanding finances. Somebody knows what that dollar amount

means. Just cannot find them. Another question for Congress?

2. **Private Health Insurance:** Employer Sponsored Insurance and other private insurance, which includes Marketplace plans.

3. **Other Health Insurance Programs:** Children's Health Insurance Program, Department of Defense, and Department of Veterans' Affairs.

4. **Medicare:** No definition provided.

5. **Medicaid:** No definition provided. Is this just the Federal government's portion or does it include state dollars too?

6. **Other Health Insurance Programs:** Includes worksite health care, other private revenues, Indian Health Service, workers' compensation, general assistance, maternal and child health, vocational rehabilitation, other federal programs, Substance Abuse and Mental Health Services Administration, other state and local programs, and school health.

7. **Other Third Party Payers:** This is a personal favorite, it only states, "Calculation of per capita estimates is not applicable" What! That is $546 Billion dollars and that is the best description we can come up with?

One of the numbers used in this book was the percent of the healthcare that was paid for by the government, state and federal. Why is this important? Because it represents the dollars that are controlled by the government Congress can influence and will ultimately affect us, the taxpayer.

Below is Table 3, expanded it to include the percent by category and I have used my own judgement as to whether the government controls a category.

Category	2018 Projected	Government	Percent
Out-of-Pocket Payments	382,700,000,000	N	10%
Private Health Insurance	1,280,400,000,000	N	34%
Medicare	767,900,000,000	Y	21%
Medicaid	621,800,000,000	Y	17%
Other Health Insurance Programs	146,400,000,000	Y	4%
Other Third Party Payers	546,500,000,000	Y	15%
	$3,745,700,000,000		

You will see that by the above definitions, 44% of the dollars are private and 57% is government sponsored.

I hope you are still with me; I am going to make a point. Next, let us look at how much each of these categories costs on an individual or per capita basis. Please not that earlier in the book I quoted $3.2 Trillion as the national spend in 2015. We have not forwarded to 2018 CMS projections where spending is now $3.7 Trillion. This is a 15.6% increase in 3 years, this is reasonable given the predicted growth rate of 5.5% per year. Even if the numbers are a bit off they are still close enough for this example of trying to get to one set of numbers that we can agree are worth working on.

Given the confusion as to the exact meaning of each category, I got rid of a few and have listed below only the categories that I felt reasonably confident that I could get good numbers for.

First just look at the Cost per Capita. This is the cost of each category based on the 2018 projections and the expected population that cost will cover.

Category	2018 Projected	Population Covered	Weight	Cost per Capita	Weighted Cost
Private Health Insurance	1,280,400,000,000	155,000,000	0.58	8,261	4,791
Medicare	767,900,000,000	53,000,000	0.20	14,489	2,898
Medicaid	621,800,000,000	57,000,000	0.22	10,909	2,400
	$2,670,100,000,000	265,000,000	1.00		10,089

Focusing on the column with the arrow, it looks like Private Health Insurance is the most cost effective at $8,261 and this would be expected because we know they cover the healthiest population. Medicare is the most expensive at $14,489, again this is not a surprise given the age of the population this program covers. With Medicaid being in the middle. If we weight the average based on population the annual cost to cover these portions of the population (265 million) is $10,089 per person.

You cannot help but notice this does not include all categories of expenditures or all the people in the country. Again, this is because I needed numbers that I could feel confident about and made sense when compared to each other. You need a numerator (top number) and a denominator (bottom number). For "Other Health

Insurance Programs" and "Other Third Party Payers" we know the numerator (dollars spent) but do not know the denominator (how many people are covered by the dollars). For "Out-of-Pocket Payments" we have the numerator and we can assume the denominator is everyone but this dollar amount is already being paid for by us and should not be included in the three categories detailed above.

I also know that that there are about 30 million people covered by Obamacare and "other forms of insurance" (the denominator) but I do not know how to get a dollar amount for the group (the numerator). The remaining 36 million, would bring the above total to 323 million, are still uninsured Even with the recent addition to the ranks of the insured we still have 36 million uninsured? Are we settling for that?

The chart above can account for $2.7 Trillion when we are spending $3.7 Trillion. What do we do with the other $1 Trillion if it is not Medicare, Medicaid or Private Insurance?

For now, let us assume the $10,089 annually per person is good for everyone in the country with the understanding that some will spend more and some less. If you multiply $10,089 by 323 Million you get $3.3 Trillion. Wait a second...we are expected to spend $3.7 Trillion in 2018, where did $400 Billion go?

By coincidence, the number $400 Billion appeared another document that passed my desk.

The Congressional Budget Office (CBO): "Since 1975, CBO has produced independent analyses of budgetary and economic issues to support the Congressional budget process. Each year, the agency's economists and budget analysts produce dozens of reports and hundreds of cost estimates for proposed legislation." *(www.cbo.gov)*

They are stated non-partisan and have produced documents about the H.R. 1628 Bill that would repeal Obamacare. The documents are easy to find but difficult to read. They also appear to work with the Joint Committee on Taxation (JCT).

Here is how the JCT defines themselves: "The Joint Committee on Taxation is a nonpartisan committee of the United States Congress, originally established under the Revenue Act of 1926. The Joint Committee operates with an experienced professional staff of Ph.D. economists, attorneys, and accountants, who assist Members of the majority and minority parties in both houses of Congress on tax legislation." *(www.jct.gov)*

Here is what both had to say about the repeal: "CBO and JCT estimate that enacting this legislation would reduce federal deficits by $420 Billion over the 2017-2026 period." And is the $420 Billion per year? Or $420 Billion over 10 years making it $42 Billion per year? It is not clear and I do not know whom to ask.

Moreover, make no mistake the cost cutting is focused on Medicaid. What about "Other Health Insurance Programs" and "Other Third Party Payers"? Why do they seem to be protected?

Enough already with the numbers, you can calculate and present them many ways to try to prove just about any point you want.

How can we make sense out of this? Businesses handle this through a budget process that matches revenues and expenses and sets a target. I have seen targets that project losses for a period of time while you bring new products or services online but over time, you cannot spend more than you have and still be an ongoing concern.

I propose we are going to have to set a target about what we are going to spend as a nation. If we do not everyone is going to say we want more. We are different. You cannot compare us to that other group.

I invite you to consider...

"When you're good at making excuses, it's hard to excel at anything else."

and...

"Adversity drives innovation."

Going back to a thought from the road...

"Everyone has to pay before healthcare will work."

You can run numbers all day and in the end, you will find more excuses than solutions. No way around it, cost is a hard problem to solve but it must be solved. There are many ways to resolve the cost issue. I propose 2 for this discussion: 1. Cut costs, 2. Capitate costs.

1. **Cut Costs:** There is waste in every system. Given we want to avoid cutting direct payments to providers; let us go back to our discussion on Indirect or Administrative costs in healthcare. This number is expressed as a percent of the total national expense for healthcare. It took a lot of

research to find a reasonable number and that number is 25% of every dollar spent goes to Indirect Cost. 25% of the projected 2018 expenditures of $3.7 Trillion are $936 Billion. You can never get rid of all it but should we at least look? Reducing the indirect costs to 20% would save $200 Billion.

2. **Capitate Payments**: With this, you essentially say here is how much money you have to take care of this population and your healthcare systems figure out how you are going to do that. In this model, taking better care of the population will save you money because they will use fewer services. In addition, it had better be good because we are going to make your report on the health of the population using those expensive health records you installed. With this model, we move from paying for sickness to paying for health. Nobody wants to be in a hospital, nobody wants to have surgery but right now providers are paid more money if people use more services.

Innovation will be driven from this revenue adversity shared by all. Everyone has to pay. There are gross inefficiencies in our system that can drive inadequate care. We have enough money to pay for healthcare for everyone. Stop making excuses and there is plenty of blame to go around; get together and fix it. Yes, I am talking to Congress and Taxpayer alike. Congress does not seem to be able to do their job. They need a nudge. Send an e-mail.

The target is our costs per person will not exceed $10,089 annually. Moreover, do not let anyone baffle you with numbers; do not let them say you do not know what you are talking about. Chances are they do not know what they are talking about.

As a last thought on cost, let us look at the Indian Health Service. It is in the category "Other Health Insurance Programs" and accounts for $5 Billion of the $146 Billion in this category. This $5 Billion covers a Native population of 2.2 million. This the buildings and all the supplies and labor involved in providing care. *(www.ihs.gov)* Using the popular per person (capita) metric this means the Indian Health Service (IHS) manages to provide care for 2.2 million for $2,318 per person.

The rest of the population we estimated $10,089 per year, that is a big difference. How is that possible? Is the IHS that good? Or is this population very underfunded? Either way we should look.

Lowest common denominator: we must eliminate as much cost as possible that does not go to direct care.

CALL TO ACTION

In this book, are included Questions for Congress. Below they are listed again with the intent that some of you mind find the time to contact your representatives and ask these questions, or other questions of your own design.

I propose we look at e-mail as a quick way to do this. Imagine if a group of people all sent the same or similar questions to their representatives. You do have to go to their site and it probably does take a little longer than a post of a tweet, but not much. Next, imagine if you bookmark the page and send one periodically, a week, a month, whatever.

If you decide to do this always be respectful, you will get farther and always be short and to the point, it might actually be read. You can just make a statement but I invite you to consider that asking a question implies that someone should respond and answer your question. Make sure it is a short and answerable question. Remember it will probably be a Congressperson's staff that will be responding.

Here are the sample questions:

Do you think term limits should be imposed on Congress?

Do you think Congress should have the same healthcare as the American people?

If Medicaid money is going to go back to the States anyway, why send it to the Feds first?

Why do we have HHS and CMS?

What does each agency do?

Between HHS and CMS there are 84,100 employees: do they all provide direct care?

If they are not providing direct care what do the employees do?

What other departments receive healthcare tax dollars that are not included in the above?

Why does each state have a different Medicaid program (customization)?

Would we save money by having each State follow the same rules (standardization)?

Given the government already spends $1.8 Trillion on healthcare how much more would it cost to cover everyone through Medicare?

We are already into healthcare for $3.2 Trillion per year. I invite you to consider Medicare as an option. In addition, if you do not want to consider it, why not?

Why aren't the blues providing legislation that would improve the Affordable Care Act?

What is your vision for healthcare?

Do you believe 100% of US citizens should have healthcare?

"Do you receive donations from for profit health insurance companies?"

"Do you receive donations from drug companies?"

"Who profits from expensive medical advances?"

"Who benefits from expensive medical advances?"

How many people are enrolled in Medicare?

How much does Medicare cost, on a yearly basis?

The last two questions I emailed our local representative in the house, Mark DeSaulnier. Below is his response

August 22, 2017

Mr. Don Livsey
1101 Reiner Lane
Walnut Creek, CA 94597

Dear Mr. Livsey:

Thank you for contacting me regarding Medicare. I appreciate you taking the time to share your thoughts with me on this important matter.

It is essential that we provide high-quality health care to Medicare and Medicaid patients. In order to ensure access to high-quality care, we must ensure that there are sufficient funds to pay for these vital programs in the future.

According to the Centers for Medicare and Medicaid Services (CMS), in 2015 Medicare spending grew to $646.2 billion. Additionally, according to CMS, as of June 2017 approximately 58.2 million people are covered by Medicare.

Again, thank you for contacting me. If I may be of assistance to you in the future, please do not hesitate to contact my office.

Sincerely,

Mark DeSaulnier
Member of Congress

Thank-you Mr. DeSaulnier for providing a prompt response to verify numbers used in this book.

EPILOGUE

What would I do if I was King? That was my first thought for the epilogue. Based on experience, discussion, and research I thought it would be easy to present the solution and it would be treated as a national epiphany. Well, that did not work out. Instead, it cannot be up to one person to provide the answers. There are too many facets, insurance, government, quality, costs, reimbursement, redundancy and misinformation. Improving the healthcare dialogue still rings true and focusing on what most of us, let's say 2/3, can agree on may be productive. The conversations must be understandable and Congress must blur the reds and the blues.

Let me end by summarizing the lowest common denominators.

Thoughts from the road...

- we got to fix it, it's broken
- Everyone should have access to healthcare.
- It needs to be affordable for all citizens.
- Everyone should contribute as a productive member of society to the best of their abilities.
- Those that make the rules need to live by the same rules.

- No one person or organization should profit excessively by exploiting the sickness of others.
- Learning from others is a strength not a weakness. This applies to both other countries as well as blue learning from red and vice versa.

A vision statement...

"The United States of America believes that a civilized and wealthy nation, such as ours, should not make the sick bear the financial burden of health care. Everyone benefits from the security and peace of mind that comes with having pre-paid insurance. The misfortune of illness, which at some time touches each one of us, is burden enough: the costs of care should be borne by society as a whole. That is why the United States wishes to re-affirm in a new Healthcare Act our commitment to the essential principle of affordable health insurance."

In order to achieve this vision we will tackle the following missions.

- We will insure 100% of the citizens of the United States.
- This insurance will be based on a uniform set of terms and conditions.

- It will be portable across all the United States
- It will provide reasonable access medically necessary services.

The next step is to get this on Amazon and sell some books. I would like to raise enough money to send a copy to all 535 Representatives and the President. Book sales will help do this and you can go to the Go Fund Me account below.

https://www.gofundme.com/improving-the-healthcare-dialogue

All proceeds will go to continue this work.

Thank you for listening.

"LET US NOT SEEK THE REPULICAN ANSWER OR THE DEMOCRATIC ANSWER, LET US NOT SEEK TO FIX THE BLAME FOR THE PAST. LET US ACCEPT OUR OWN RESPONSIBILITY FOR THE FUTURE."